THE MENTAL EDGE

GETTING THE MOST OUT OF THE MARTIAL ARTS

Loren W. Christensen

Royce Publications

Canadian Cataloguing in Publication Data

Christensen, Loren W. (Loren Wayne), 1946-
  The mental edge

Bibliography: p.
ISBN 0-7740-3819-5

1. Martial arts.   2. Martial arts—Psychological aspects.   I. Title.

GV1101.C57 1989   796.8   C89-094157-2

Printed and bound in Canada

1 2 3 4 5   93 92 91 90 89

Dedication

To Carrie, Daniel and Amy. Choose paths that are challenging, and walk them with courage, compassion and honour.

Acknowledgements

Special thanks to my senior black belt, Gary Sussman, for his patience and skill behind the camera. For their time in front of the camera, I would like to thank students Scott Wong, Amy Christensen, Russ Weaver, Brian Roth, Dexter Reed, Ronda Vanyi, and Geary Lockard.

Make the mind command the body—never let the body command the mind.

General George Patton

CONTENTS

v

About the Author

Loren W. Christensen began studying karate in 1965 and has since broadened his study of the martial arts to include kung fu, tai chi, jujitsu, judo and arnis. Loren holds black belt ranking in the Filipino martial art of arnis, awarded by Professor Remy Presas, and a fifth-degree black belt in karate, awarded by the American Teachers Association of the Martial Arts.

Loren has been a law enforcement officer since 1967, serving as a military policeman in Vietnam and presently as a police officer in Portland, Oregon. Because of the nature of his work, his approach to the martial arts is practical and realistic. He occasionally competes in karate tournaments and has been rated by *Karate Illustrated* magazine as a Region 1, Top Ten forms competitor and a Top Ten weapons competitor.

In addition to teaching at the Mushin School of Karate in Portland, Loren has taught in many seminars, law enforcement organizations, and colleges. He has written dozens of articles for martial arts magazines and two previous books, *An Introduction to Defensive Tactics for Law Enforcement Officers* and *The Way Alone: Your Path to Excellence in the Martial Arts*.

Loren W. Christensen

Introduction

"WHAT IS YOUR GREATEST weapon?" The master asked the young man.
  The student scratched his head and pondered the question. "My fists are my greatest weapon, sir."
  "Wrong!" snapped the master. "Think again."
  "Well. . ." The student rubbed his chin and furrowed his brow. Suddenly his face lit. "I know master. My kicks!"
  "Wrong!" The master's patience was growing thin. "Use your head. Think. What is your greatest weapon?"
  The student's frightened eyes darted about the room and settled on a sword. "My weapons, master, my weapons." His face glowed with his enlightenment.
  "Wrong!" shouted the master. He reached toward the frightened pupil and lightly smacked the top of his head. "It is here. In your head. Learn to use your mind and you will never be defeated."

I began studying karate in 1965. Although I've been studying for a long time, only in the last few years have I discovered my greatest weapon. Of course, my mind has been there all along—but it was undisciplined and floundering, effective only when I thought to use it.

  I believe my progression as a martial artist has been typical. During the first several years I emphasized learning and developing technique. By the time I earned my first black belt in 1970, I'd devoted much of my time to perfecting the mechanics of karate: power, speed, form, and accurate application.

For the next several years I trained to develop discipline. I worked to develop a will so strong that nothing could prevent me from reaching any goal, no matter how difficult. To develop this trait, I practised repetitions. Lots of repetitions. There were workouts so strenuous that my legs would give out and my arms would ache and twitch so much that I was unable to sleep. But no matter how sore, injured or sick, I continued to set goals, often unrealistically, and trained until I reached them. There were times when I would perform a thousand backfists or throw side kicks around a quarter-mile track, when my muscles were completely exhausted and in great pain. But I continued, digging deep into myself to bring out a little more energy and a little more strength. From this I developed a curiosity about the power of the mind. I was amazed at what I could do just by mental fortitude. I wanted to investigate further.

I began reading everything I could find about the application of mental skills to physical performance, especially books and magazine articles on the mental training of our Olympic champions. I talked with hypnotists, acupuncturists, physical therapists, marathon runners, bodybuilders, skiers and several masters of the martial arts. I was suprised, in the beginning, to discover many similarities in the way these diverse disciplines view the mind. Later, however, as I became more aware of how the mind is used, I realized that certain mental skills are basic to any physical endeavour that requires speed, power and coordination of the mind and body.

This book contains many techniques I have found to be the most effective in my teachings, writings and personal training. Although I have used them for a number of years, I'm still amazed at how well they work for me and am always pleased to hear enthusiastic students praise their value.

I like to think of the techniques in this book as a North American approach to mental training in the martial arts. Not having been raised in Japan or China, I can offer few insights into the Asian point of view.

The mental techniques in this book are simple and easy to understand. Occasionally some ideas may seem to contradict others. For example, the chapter on mushin teaches keeping the mind clear of thought during battle, while the chapter on mental preparedness encourages alertness and the development of a fight plan. With careful reading and experimentation you will discover that the two skills complement each other.

The techniques, concepts and disciplines in this book will radically affect the way you think and progress in the martial arts. The methods described are based on my own learning, practice and experimentation. I am not a psychologist or a hypnotist, but simply a martial artist looking for the mental edge.

1

RELAXATION

MENTAL RELAXATION

THE MENTAL EXERCISES discussed in the following chapters are most effective when the mind and body are relaxed. When the mind is relaxed and under control, it is far more susceptible to self-suggestion and positive visualization. The busy, agitated or preoccupied mind will receive little if any benefit from such exercises.

If you were to toss a rock into churning, pounding ocean surf, the rock would disappear without visible effect. But if you were to toss a rock into a clear, still lake, you would hear the "ka-thunk," see the splash and watch small ripples spread into larger ones.

It's the same with your mind. If you are agitated, stressed or thinking about other things, your mind will be like the roaring sea, and any self-suggestion will disappear in your own turbulence. If you are relaxed, however, and calm as the still lake, your suggestions will sink in quickly, deeply and produce noticeable results.

THE PHYSICALLY RELAXED FIGHTER

Generally, the tense, stiff and tight fighter will have one major problem—an inability to fight. When the mind is in turmoil, like the churning sea, the body reflects that condition and loses its ability to generate speed, explosiveness, flexibility and strength. At the same time, the agitated mind experiences difficulty perceiving, reacting and adapting. Tension blocks the mind and body and keeps them from performing at their best.

MUSCULAR TENSION

I am very much in favour of weight training as a supplement to karate training. However, people who train a great deal with weights, especially bodybuilders, tend to flex their muscles while executing karate techniques. This
may be because they are conscious of their development and feel they must
show their strength by flexing their arms and chest.

Tensing their muscles may reveal their muscular development, but it
doesn't enhance their karate. In fact, this habit is detrimental. Movement,
especially fast movement, requires a sharp contraction of the muscles in the
limb that is moving. Throwing a backfist, for example, calls into play all the
muscles in the upper back, shoulders, upper arms, and those around the
elbow. To propel the backfist with speed requires these muscles to contract
(or tense) sharply. If the muscle fibres are already tensed, few are left to
contribute explosively to the backfist. If, say, eighty percent of the fibres are
used up even before the technique is launched, the result will be a slow and
stiff backfist.

Tension increases fatigue. When you are mentally and physically tense,
your energy dissipates at an accelerated rate. You will experience such
symptoms as heavy legs, slow reflexes and burning lungs, all of which
diminish your ability to perform at your best.

MENTAL TENSION

You don't have to be a bodybuilder to have tense, tight muscles. When you
are mentally tense, whether from fear, stress or any number of other causes,
your muscles will tense up as if you are purposely flexing them. This produces
ineffective techniques.

Relaxed, you will not only think more clearly and have greater speed and
strength, but will more easily control such emotions as fear and anger. As a
result, you'll be the master of yourself and the situation.

Practise the following relaxation exercises regularly. The more you practise
them, the easier it will be to bring on the relaxed condition. In a short time,
you will reap the many benefits of relaxation in your everyday life and in
your martial arts training.

RELAXATION EXERCISES

Although there are many relaxation exercises, for our purposes here I've
narrowed down my personal list to five.

Since it may take time to get a feel for a relaxation exercise, don't discard
it until you have experimented with it over several days. Otherwise you may
toss out an exercise prematurely that could possibly be beneficial.

Some people will find one exercise they like and use only that one. They
prefer the consistency of using the same exercise each session, finding their
minds become conditioned to respond to the one. Others, myself included,
prefer to have several to choose from because on certain days the mind reacts
better to one approach than to another.

Method I: Blue Fog

Put on light, loose-fitting clothes, and find a quiet place where you'll be comfortable. Lie down on a bed or sofa that offers good support and place a small pillow under your head. If you have lower-back problems you may want to place another pillow under your knees to relieve back stress. Do not cross your feet. Let your hands rest comfortably on your lower abdomen. If you fall asleep too easily in this position, sit in a comfortable chair that offers good support.

Close your eyes and allow your body to sink heavily into whatever you are sitting or lying on. Breathe in through your nose, drawing the air slowly and deeply into your lower abdomen. Your inhalation should take about six seconds. Hold the breath for three seconds and then exhale to a count of six seconds. One complete breath, therefore, takes a total of fifteen seconds.

There should be no strain in this procedure. If initially you feel your inhalation is complete at three seconds, that's fine. But strive to slow the pace to six seconds inhaling and six seconds exhaling. After practising this exercise you will eventually time your breaths correctly.

After just a few breaths you may begin to experience a mild calming effect throughout your body. To enhance this, visualize the incoming air as a cool, blue fog entering through your nose, tumbling and swirling down your lungs into your abdomen, thighs and feet. As you hold your breath for three seconds, picture the fog tumbling throughout your body, cooling and calming. Then slowly exhale, imagining the fog traveling the same course back out your nostrils. As it exits, it turns red—the result of collecting such negative elements as fatigue, tension, anger and frustration. As you release these poisons with each exhalation, feel yourself sink deeper and deeper into a state of relaxation.

Lie comfortably, with your legs uncrossed and your hands resting on your abdomen. Do not interlock your fingers.

If you fall asleep when lying down, sit in a comfortable chair with your back straight and your hands resting on your knees.

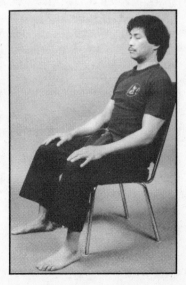

Method II: Progressive Muscle Relaxation

This method involves a progressive and systematic relaxation of all the major muscle groups: neck, shoulders, arms, chest, abdomen, buttocks, thighs, calves and feet. Your objective is to tense and relax each major body part until you are completely bathed with a sensation of warm relaxation.

Assume a comfortable position on the floor or in your favourite chair. As with Method I, the room should be quiet and comfortable and your clothing should not constrict your breathing. Repeat a few deep inhalations and exhalations to help you settle into your position.

Begin by visualizing your feet. See and feel them in your mind: the toes, the arches and the heels. Focus all your attention on them as you tense them as hard as you can. Abruptly stop the muscle contractions and enjoy the pleasurable, soothing sensations in your feet.

Move up to your calves, visualizing every inch of them for a moment. Then tense them hard for ten seconds. Relax the tension and again feel the pleasurable relaxation that sweeps over the muscles. (**Caution:** the calf muscles may be susceptible to painful cramping when doing this exercise. If this happens to your calves, or any muscle group, stop the tension immediately and concentrate on relaxing the muscle.)

After you've relaxed the calves, move on to the thighs, buttocks and all the muscle groups up to the face. Repeat the same order as with the feet and calves: awareness, contraction, and abrupt relaxation with each muscle group. You may want to segment your body parts further: lower back, forearms, hands, and various parts of your face. Many people, especially those having trouble relaxing, find that visualizing additional body parts is more beneficial.

Each body part should receive about ten seconds of tensing and then five to ten seconds of relaxing before you move on to the next section. The entire body shouldn't take more than ten minutes to relax. Remember to breathe slowly and deeply as you progressively relax your muscles.

When you have completed visualizing your entire body, take a few minutes to enjoy the sensation of total relaxation.

Method III: Neutral Bath

This easy method of inducing relaxation is very pleasurable and can be practised virtually every day. All that's needed is a warm bathroom and a bathtub filled with water at approximately the same temperature as your body—37°C (98.6°F). By submerging yourself into this "neutral" water, you'll quickly be lulled into a relaxed state.

The neutral bath works because of the way the skin surface, which is covered with nerve endings, reacts to stimulus. Many of the skin's nerve endings are cold receptors and when water that is colder than your body makes contact with them, the sympathetic nervous system produces a physiological reaction, such as goosebumps, shivering, or even shock. On the other hand, water that is the same temperature as the body has a soothing effect on the nerve receptors and the overall nervous system.

Years ago, before tranquilizers were developed, a neutral bath was commonly used to calm an agitated mental patient, who might be submerged for several hours. But you don't need to sit in the tub for several hours to relax yourself. Try it for about thirty minutes at the end of your school or work day or whenever you want the sedative effect of a neutral bath. Pick up a good thermometer at any pharmacy and make sure the water is maintained between 36° and 37°C (96°–98°F) the entire time you're submerged. The air temperature in your bathroom should be high enough to avoid any coolness on your body.

Although you may choose to have a neutral bath every day, you should never have one prior to a workout, as it will drain your energy. The bath will have a wonderful sedative effect that will relax your muscles, calm your mind and prepare you for your breathing and self-suggestion exercises (Chapter 3).

Method IV: Six Gate Breathing

I was taught this exercise several years ago by an acupuncturist and it has remained one of my favourites. I like the combination of breathing and mental imagery, which quickly relaxes and soothes my nerves. The name refers to the body's six entrance and exit points where, according to Chinese traditional medicine, breath is exchanged: the palms, the soles of the feet, the navel and nose. Of course you can't really breathe through five of these points; therefore, you must visualize the process.

Begin by assuming a comfortable position, lying or sitting. Close your eyes, slowly and deeply inhale and visualize a blue, swirling fog entering through the soles of your feet. The fog tumbles upward through the calves, thighs, abdomen, chest, arms, neck, and into the head. Your inhalation should be slow and steady until your entire body is filled.

When your inhalation is complete, take a moment to visualize the cool fog and feel it calm and relax your body. Then as you exhale, imagine the fog turning red as it collects your tension and fatigue. It moves downward from your head and joins the fog flowing upward from your hands and arms. From your shoulders it pours through your chest, abdomen, pelvis, thighs, calves and out the soles of your feet. The exhalation should be slow and steady until the fog completely leaves your body.

Your hands make up the next two gates. Inhale and visualize the fog entering through your palms, moving up your arms, into your head and then downward, filling all parts of your body. Pause for a few moments to enjoy the calming sensation, then, beginning with your feet, reverse the order as you exhale.

Your navel is the next gate. Inhale and let the fog fill your abdomen and flow over into the other parts of your body. Proceed as with the other gates.

The sixth gate is your nose. Breathe in and picture the fog swirling downward to fill all of your body. Follow the same procedure as with the other gates.

Some teachers recommend breathing in through the nose and exhaling from the mouth, while others suggest inhaling and exhaling through the nose. I don't find any differences. Try both methods and use the one you find more effective.

Method V: Key Word

The last method is a quick way to achieve relaxation after you have gained expertise with one or all of these methods. Once you have some experience with self-suggestion (Chapter 3), you can cue yourself to relax immediately whenever you say a specific word. This will be your key word.

The word you choose can be any you like, such as "relax," "calm," "tension out." I use my middle name, Wayne. It works well for me because I rarely hear it and use only my middle initial when I write my name. Perhaps best of all, I can remember it.

The process of planting a key word into your subconscious will be explained in greater detail in Chapter 4.

When you have found a method and an exercise that suits you, practise it once, preferably twice a day in a quiet place. Eventually, as you become adept at self-induced relaxation, you'll be able to practise it unnoticed just about anywhere at any time: standing in line, sitting in a meeting or even while driving a car. The depth of this relaxation will certainly not be as great as it is when you are in a quiet setting, but you will be able to achieve a level of relaxation that calms the mind and soothes the body.

A WAR STORY

The first time I realized the benefits of instant relaxation was when, as a police officer, I arrived at the scene of a civil disobedience and found myself facing an angry mob of about 150 people who were trying to get into a government building. Although the mob consisted of two groups with divergent political views, they quickly joined forces when the police arrived. There was pushing and screaming, and several arrests were made.

At one point, I was blocking the door to the building while the crowd screamed and threatened me. I felt a little like Custer must have at his last stand. I was breathing as if I'd been running sprints, my eyes were watering and my hands were trembling. I remembered my relaxation exercises. Although this was not the quiet and peaceful setting I was used to, I began breathing slowly and rhythmically. Keeping my eyes on the crowd, I tried to visualize the cooling, calming oxygen flowing in and out of my lungs. In a matter of moments, I was calmed, relaxed and able to control myself and the dangerous situation.

The bottom line of this anecdote is that the more you practise, the easier the exercise becomes and the more comfortable you will be doing it in less than ideal surroundings.

Whether you always choose the same relaxation method or prefer a variety of ways, relaxation will help you physically as well as mentally. In addition, deep relaxation is an absolute prerequisite for self-suggestion and visualization exercises.

2

CONSCIOUS AND SUBCONSCIOUS MIND

I NEVER ALLOW MY students to begin a sentence with the words, "I can't." The moment someone slips and says, "I can't do that kick" or, "I can't get this hand technique," I reprimand them immediately. I remind them that we have a rule never to utter those two words. If they are having trouble with something I prefer them to ask, "Could you please help me with this kick?" or, "May I have assistance with this hand technique?"

Why make such a big deal out of two little words? Because every time you say "I can't," there is a part of you listening—your subconscious mind. Even when you just whisper "I can't," your subconscious is right there listening in and getting the message that you can't do something. After a while, your subconscious begins to believe that you can't do it and starts directing your body to respond accordingly. Even if you didn't intend your statement seriously but were merely trying to get someone to disagree and compliment you, your subconscious mind has been listening and believing. It's rather like a computer, in that it doesn't understand indirect statements or jokes, but accepts everything it hears literally.

THE TWO-PART MIND

Rest assured you have only one mind. However, it possesses two parts, each with individual characteristics, distinct abilities and functions. These two parts go by a variety of names. Waking mind and sleeping mind are the most descriptive, but the most commonly accepted terms are conscious and subconscious mind.

Your conscious mind is your reasoning mind. It's always busy choosing. It chose this book you're reading, that soda pop you're drinking and the chair you're sitting on. As you go about your day, your conscious mind uses your knowledge, your experience and your five senses to make choices.

Your subconscious mind deals with your environment using such instincts as self-preservation and aggression. Your instinct for self-preservation may sometimes cause you to feel fear, act selfishly or in ways that may embarrass you and cause you to wonder what happened.

Your subconscious mind accepts everything you imprint upon it as true and will then go about bringing that truth back to you in the form of experience. For example, if you consciously say and think often enough that you can't do something, your subconscious mind will believe every word and then substantiate that belief by directing your actions so that you can't do it.

Even at an early age, the subconscious mind accepts everything imprinted on it as the truth. Positive teaching, in and out of the karate school, will help the child progress as a martial artist and as a person.

Control of the Conscious Mind

Your subconscious mind is vulnerable to suggestions and impressions fed to it by your conscious mind. But since the subconscious doesn't analyze information, you need to monitor carefully what goes in.

Think of your conscious mind as a guard working to protect your subconscious from negative and erroneous information. You must be aware of what happens in your conscious mind so that your subconscious is fed data that are positive, happy, constructive and peaceful. If your thinking is full of "I can't" and other negative or self-destructive thoughts, you'll need to take steps now to change this pattern to enable your subconscious to guide you in a positive direction, not only as a martial artist but as a human being.

THE POWER OF SUGGESTION

Here is an example of how powerful a conscious suggestion can be on the subconscious mind. One of my students, an excellent kata performer, was recently training hard on a new kata in preparation for an upcoming tournament. She was experiencing a problem of blanking out about two-thirds of the way through the form. Every time she got to the jump front kick, her mind would stop and she couldn't remember the next move. When I reminded her, she would finish the form without any further problem.

I told her to practise that part of the form over and over so that she would flow smoothly from the jump kick into the next movement. She drilled on the section countless times until she could perform the entire kata without freezing after the front kick. Two days before the tournament her form looked great, and I was convinced she would win her division.

The day of the tournament, however, she arrived worried that she would again freeze after the jump kick. The more she talked about it the more she was convinced she would draw a blank. I talked to her at length, trying to convince her that her form was in great shape, and the problem was now in the past. But the closer the time came for her to compete, the more negative she became. The harder I tried to convince her she would do well, the more she told herself she would fail.

And so she did.

When they called her name, she bowed and began her kata with strong, crisp movements. But when she executed that jump front kick, she froze. She stood there for a moment, a blank look on her face and then with great embarrassment, she bowed to the judges and left the ring.

She did exactly as she said she would because, by having expressed over and over that she would freeze, she had implanted the suggestion in her subconscious mind. When she performed the kata, she did exactly as she had programmed herself.

Remember, the subconscious mind accepts all its information literally. Even though this student didn't wish to freeze in front of all those people and embarrass herself, she had unintentionally set herself up for that response. On the other hand, if she had given her subconscious mind positive information to flow smoothly from the jump kick to the next move, she would have performed accordingly. Remember: the subconscious mind doesn't care one way or the other. It gives direction based only on the information it has.

A Dirty Trick Foiled

Not everyone is susceptible to negative suggestion. Just minutes before our division was to compete, I reminded a nationally ranked kata competitor of a leg injury he had received at that same tournament the year before. I asked if he remembered the great pain he had been in and suggested that the cast, which had been on his leg for three months, must have dramatically weakened his leg muscles. I pointed out there was slim chance the leg had fully recovered, and that he might easily injure it again in the competition. (OK, I admit it was a cheap trick.)

He won first place, and I got second.

His subconscious conditioning was such that my suggestions didn't work. Although he had experienced a bad injury the year before, he had recuperated physically and mentally. Most importantly, he had no doubt in his mind about his ability to compete. My attempt to draw out worry from his subconscious only brought out his self-confidence. A suggestion cannot sway the subconscious against the will of the conscious mind. In this case, the champion's conscious mind rejected my negative suggestions because the man had convinced himself his leg was in top shape.

The subconscious mind is incredibly vast: everything you've ever seen or heard is recorded there. People under hypnosis have recalled details from as early in their lives as three months of age. They've been able to describe their nursery down to the pictures on the wall, the colour of the rug and even repeat conversations that took place in their presence. Of course, at three months they didn't understand what they were seeing or hearing, but since it was all recorded on the "video tape" of their subconscious minds, they were able to "replay" these events years later under hypnosis.

Throughout this book we'll be discussing various ways to tap into the subconscious mind to help you progress in karate. With a greater understanding of your mind, especially the subconscious, you'll be able to program it with the information you want it to have: information that will give you positive results.

DON'T THINK SO MUCH

Sometimes your brain gets in the way of your physical performance. By being too analytical of each step of a technique, you can miss the entire movement. I've found that students who think analytically at the wrong time have difficulty learning. As a teacher it can be frustrating because I know the student can do it, but his or her learning is blocked by overanalysis.

In the martial art of modern arnis, the founder, Professor Remy Presas, teaches a basic twelve-count striking drill with the rattan stick. As the name implies, twelve offensive blows are delivered to twelve vulnerable targets. The drill is designed so that each strike flows smoothly into the next and continues in succession through all twelve attacks.

When I first began teaching the basic twelve strikes, I broke each movement down into precise directions of force, footwork patterns, body motion and the various technical aspects of the striking hand. I quickly discovered this rather simple drill took several classes to teach because of the students' confusion over the complexity of the movements. To be painfully honest, they were confused because of the way I was teaching the drill.

One night I decided to teach it a different way to a small group of new students. Actually it was not a new way at all, but the way I was initially taught by Professor Presas. I had learned it quickly his way, but later, when I began to teach it, I reverted back to my old style of teaching.

My "new" way was to tell my students not to try and analyze the twelve strikes. Instead, they were told to emulate my motions and not think about what I was doing at all.

I then slowly led them through the drill without giving them any explanation as to what they were doing. There was some confusion at first because most of them wanted to analyze the drill. Without giving them a chance to reflect on what they had done, I had them follow me through a second time. By the third time, they gave up trying to analyze what I was doing because I wasn't giving them time for analysis. By the fourth time, they were beginning to emulate my movements. By the seventh or eighth time, most were doing a very good job of copying my technique. The students had achieved in five minutes what had taken me four days to teach using my old method.

I spent the next fifteen minutes explaining body positioning, foot work, flowing and so on. By the end of the class, the students not only could do the striking drill but also had a good understanding of its mechanics.

Be Like the Child

Children are the easiest group to teach. It's true they don't concentrate as well as adults, but they have another trait that makes tolerating their horseplay worthwhile: they learn at an extraordinary speed. This is primarily because they don't analyze what they are learning. They don't break down the material, put it into little categories and label everything. Children simply see the teacher do it and they emulate—no questions asked.

To be the best you can be, there comes a time when you have to keep your thinking quiet and just let your body perform naturally. Whether you're learning a kick, a combination or a kata, emulate first and think about all the details later.

Try it and discover what the children already know.

Children do not analyze, they emulate. Sometimes you can learn faster by just doing it. There is plenty of time to think about it later.

3

SELF-SUGGESTION

WE ARE ALL SUSCEPTIBLE to suggestion, whether it comes from another person or from ourselves. When you practise self-suggestion, the cues come from you and are heard only by you. The old saying "you can talk yourself in or out of anything" sums up what self-suggestion is all about. By talking to yourself, you can effectively influence both your thinking and your behaviour.

Unknowingly, our minds are constantly being stimulated by suggestions from powerful outside sources. You may have had no idea you wanted a chocolate bar until you saw a candy display rack by the grocery cash register. You didn't realize what a junker you drove until you saw that shiny red sports car down at Biff's Used Cars. And a slick beer advertisement on TV can get you hankering not just for a brew, but for good times and the good life—just like those guys and gals on the tube. Indeed, suggestions of all sorts bombard our minds all day long.

Self-suggestion is even more powerful. But since you're giving the directions, you have total control over the process. There is nothing mysterious about it, since it is based on the natural relationship between the conscious and subconscious mind. With an understanding of how to make self-suggestion work for you, your karate and your life will benefit in wondrous ways.

We are going to examine self-suggestion as a method of using the mind to improve your fighting art in the following ways:

● Erasing fears and self-doubts
● Breaking undesirable habits

- Increasing your physical skill
- Increasing your ability to learn
- Improving your competitive performance

THE PROCEDURE

Although the following process may seem complicated at first, it will get easier the more you practise it. You'll soon become enthusiastic about self-suggestion as you discover how it can help you improve your fighting technique, as well as set you on a course of continual improvement and success beyond what you thought possible.

The first step in the process of self-suggestion is to know what it is you wish to improve. In order to have a clear picture of your objectives, form a list of all the things you wish to accomplish in your martial arts study.

- I wish to feel more confident in tournament competition
- I wish to improve my sparring
- I wish to improve my kata
- I wish to develop greater self-confidence
- I wish to earn a black belt

Your list may look similar to this one or it may look different altogether. What is important is that you carefully analyze yourself and create a list specific to your needs and wants.

Get Relaxed

Self-suggestion is most effective when you are physically and mentally relaxed. Refer to the relaxation exercises in Chapter 1 and experiment with them to determine one (or more) that works well for you. Find a comfortable, quiet place and get your body and mind into a deep state of relaxation.

The Suggestible State of Mind

You've taken ten or fifteen minutes to achieve a state of relaxation and you are feeling a soothing calm, a heaviness, as all your tensions melt away. As you breathe deeply, you will experience a wonderful feeling of warmth and an almost indescribable sensation that some people call "letting go." You'll feel as if you are bordering on sleep, but your mind will remain alert and your subconscious ready to receive suggestions.

Do not take any shortcuts with the relaxation exercises in your eagerness to get to the suggestions. Remember, your mind and body must be in a deep state of relaxation to be receptive.

The Eyelid Test

You're now going to conduct a simple, painless experiment to determine how susceptible you are to the power of suggestion.

You've already achieved a deep state of relaxation, so stay exactly where you are. Fix your eyes on a small object, such as a spot or a tack on the wall. This object should be directly in front of you, at eye level, so that there is no strain.

Now let your conscious mind suggest to your subconscious that you close your eyes and keep them closed. Your goal in this exercise is to close your eyes involuntarily, but if this doesn't happen right away, don't be concerned. You're probably not relaxed enough and will need to work more on that next time. In the meanwhile, close your eyes anyway and proceed as though you were in a suggestible state. Just the act of pretending that it's happening will help you close your eyes involuntarily the next time you practise.

Following are some of the suggestions that I use for the eye test. It's unnecessary to memorize them. They are presented here just to give you an idea of the possible wording and the process.

These suggestions should be made silently rather than vocalized. If you are having trouble concentrating, you may soundlessly mouth the words.

"Now that I'm deeply relaxed, I'm going to count slowly to ten and my eyelids will grow heavy, watery and tired. My eyes may even want to close before I complete my count to ten. When my eyes close, I'll be in a suggestible state. I'll be fully conscious, hear everything and be able to give suggestions to my subconscious mind. One . . . my eyelids are becoming heavy . . . Two . . . My eyes are becoming watery . . . Three . . . My eyelids are growing tired and heavy . . . Four . . . I can hardly keep my eyes open . . . Five . . . My eyes are beginning to close . . . Six . . . My eyes are so heavy . . . Seven . . . I'm relaxed . . . Eight . . . I can't keep my eyelids open . . . Nine . . . My eyelids are closed . . . I'm in a suggestible state . . . Ten . . . I'm now susceptible to whatever suggestions I wish."

These suggestions should be made slowly and with pauses between each so that your mind has time to absorb them. Take your time and repeat some of them if necessary. Remember to maintain your deep, rhythmic breathing throughout the entire session. For example, you can pause after "I can't keep my eyelids open" and perform three or four repetitions of deep breathing as you feel your eyes closing. With each exhalation your eyelids sag lower and lower.

The Tingling Hand Test

Here is a second test you can try. Its purpose is the same as that of the eyelid test, to examine your receptivity to suggestion. You may use the same basic dialogue.

"I'm completely relaxed. As I slowly count to ten and even before I get to ten, I'll experience a tingling or numbness in my right hand. One . . . I'm concentrating on my right hand . . . I can see it in my mind . . . it's completely relaxed . . . Two . . . I'm beginning to feel a pleasant tingling sensation in my hand . . . Three . . . I can see my hand in my mind's eye . . . it's relaxed . . . limp . . . heavy . . . relaxed . . . Four . . . I'm relaxed . . . Five . . . My hand is beginning to tingle . . . tingle . . . tingle . . . Six . . .

It's a pleasant feeling . . . I'm relaxed . . . I feel heavy . . . my hand is tingling . . . Seven . . . It's tingling more now . . . it's becoming stronger . . . Eight . . . It's an enjoyable sensation . . . Nine . . . It's really tingling now . . . tingling . . . tingling . . . Ten . . . I'm now in a suggestible state and receptive to suggestions."

If your mind is receptive in both tests, your eyelids will close and your hand will tingle. If it doesn't happen the first time, it's important not to be overconcerned. The next time you try, be sure you're completely relaxed and concentrating on what you are doing. You must believe that it will happen. Tell yourself over and over that it will happen. Remember, the name of the game here is self-suggestion.

Once your eyes are closed, you can proceed with other suggestions. The tingling in your hand, however, should be stopped so that you can proceed without any distractions. Use the following suggestions:

"The tingling in my hand will go away . . . My hand will return to normal . . . I realize I've reached a deep suggestible state . . . My entire body is relaxed . . . every muscle . . . I like the sensation . . . The tingling in my hand has stopped . . . I'm now ready to give suggestions to my subconscious mind."

Your eyelids will open automatically when you come out of the suggestible state.

IMPROVING KARATE WITH SELF-SUGGESTION

Refer to the list you made regarding the things you wanted to improve or accomplish in karate. Prioritize is so that the first item you want to work on is at the top, which in this case is "I wish to feel more confident in tournament competition."

Notice how positively this statement is structured. By thinking and speaking positively, you're already on your way toward improvement. Even if you're scared to death of competition, never speak, write or think of it in negative terms, because when you say, "I'm afraid of tournaments," you actually release negative energy and reinforce negative memories of tournament experiences. If you've never been in a tournament, your negative expression will feed into your imagined fears.

IT IS IMPORTANT TO YOUR SUCCESS IN KARATE THAT YOU THINK, SPEAK AND ACT IN A POSITIVE MANNER AND DIRECT ALL SUCH ACTIVITY TOWARD A SOLUTION.

When you're first learning self-suggestion, your mind will work most efficiently with just one item at a time. Since tournament competition involves kata, sparring, judging, demonstrations and promotion, let's narrow your objective even further and just deal with improving your tournament fighting. Concentrate on this for a few days and then add other objectives as you begin to experience progress and comfort in the process.

Analyzing Your Objective

You are now ready to analyze your objective. In this case you want to discover what it is you wish to change about your feelings toward tournament fighting. This is best accomplished while in the suggestible state.

Place yourself in a deeply relaxed state and test your susceptibility with either the eyelid test or the tingling hand test. When you are ready, give yourself the suggestion that you are now prepared to analyze your feelings toward tournament competition. Then ask yourself a series of questions, for example:

1. What are my feelings about getting hurt?
2. What are my feelings about being embarrassed in front of my peers?
3. What are my feelings toward specific competitors?
4. What are my feelings toward competing in front of large crowds?
5. What are my feelings about losing?
6. What are my feelings toward winning?
7. What are my feelings about my physical condition?
8. What are my feelings about putting my reputation on the line?

These are tough questions to ask yourself. Your conscious mind may not always know the answers and even if it did, it may not be completely honest with you. Many of the truths lie buried in your subconscious but will emerge as you analyze yourself in the relaxed, suggestible state.

You'll sometimes be amazed at the honesty of the answers and perhaps a little shocked at some of the things you'll discover about yourself. You may not always like some of the answers, but at least they're now out in the open—in the privacy of your own mind—where you can deal with them.

Consider one question at a time and try to think of as many answers as you can. Take your time with the questions and answers, mulling them over in your mind. Ponder the answers and try to consider every angle. Look at everything that bubbles to the surface from your subconscious. Frequently, what at first appears to be ridiculous will turn out to be significant to your problem and, perhaps, offer a solution.

When you rouse yourself from your relaxed state, write down as many of the answers and solutions as possible in a notebook. Divide your notebook into two sections: the first to log your answers and a second section to list what you are going to do to improve yourself. The act of writing helps to solidify your thinking as well as provide quick reference and an organized plan of correction.

Through self-suggestion and listing your findings and solutions, your mind will begin moving you toward improvement. As you gradually realize results, you will gather strength from them to improve even more.

Positive Suggestions Only

Physical limitations aside, your problems are more than likely the result of having continuously fed yourself negative information over an extended period of time. If you continuously tell yourself that you can't do something or that you are afraid to do it—"I can't fight well in a tournament" or "I'm afraid I'll get hurt"—your subconscious will accept this information without weighing its validity one way or the other. It will then simply direct your actions in such a way as to reinforce the information it has stored.

Once you have taken the opportunity through self-suggestion to analyze yourself and your problem(s), you are then ready to begin thinking positively. Imagine that your mind is a video tape on which you've recorded an old movie. You're tired of that same old movie because you've seen it a hundred times and you're not getting anything out of it. To get rid of it you either erase it or tape another program over it. Erasing the old information and leaving the new is exactly what you'll be doing in your mind, by wiping out the old negativism and replacing it with positive thoughts.

Let's say that one of the major problems you discovered as you analyzed your feelings about tournament competition was an anxiety about competing in front of crowds. List this in your notebook. On your solution page write positive statements, such as:

1. I love fighting in front of crowds.
2. I use their presence as a source of dynamic energy to give me awesome strength and blinding speed.
3. My thunderous punches and pile-driving kicks will thrill the audience.
4. If I make a mistake in front of them, I realize this is part of my growth and I will learn from it.
5. My body is filled with an electric energy that will ignite the crowd, create thrilling excitement, and bring cheers.
6. I feel positive about the butterflies in my stomach and think of them as charging me with energy and anticipation.
7. I am a performer, a star, a warrior, ready to thrill the crowd with the beauty and precision of my karate.

Notice that these affirmations are embellished with such descriptive adjectives as "thunderous," "thrilling" and "dynamic." Highly descriptive words communicate intense feeling and greatly influence your subconscious mind.

Self-suggestion and Positive Statements

Your next step is to imprint these affirmations into your subconscious mind. As before, induce deep relaxation, test yourself with the eyelid or hand test and make your positive statements. Take your time. Pause between the various affirmations to inhale deeply and exhale slowly, visualizing the words being absorbed into your subconscious.

Enjoy the relaxed sensation that has enveloped your body. Repeat often that you are relaxed, calm and receptive to the statements, and be sure you understand what you are saying and are not just repeating empty words. This is especially important if you repeat a sentence two or three times.

Always make statements in the present tense because the subconscious has difficulty dealing with the past and future. Instead of saying, "Next week at the tournament" say, "As I prepare to fight, the butterflies in my stomach are charging me with great energy and strength." Use the present tense even though your tournament may be a week away.

Awakening from Self-suggestion

After you have completed your suggestions, tell yourself that on the count of five you'll fully awaken. "In a moment I'm going to count slowly from five to one and on the count of one I'll awaken completely refreshed, alert, and responsive to my suggestions . . . Five . . . I'm beginning to return to normal . . . Four . . . I'm awakening . . . Three . . . My eyes are opening . . . Two . . . My eyes are open . . . One . . . I'm fully awake, refreshed and responsive to my suggestions."

After you return to your normal consciousness, sit quietly for a few moments and enjoy the feeling of peace that has enveloped you. You may feel a lightness in your body as if your arms may drift upward. There's a clarity and calmness in your mind. You may have a feeling of greater control over your mind as there will be fewer rambling thoughts bouncing about. It's a wonderful feeling; pause and enjoy it.

DEVELOPING CONFIDENCE

Self-suggestion can be used to inject an attitude of confidence into your subconscious so that daily training and competition are met in a positive manner, rather than with self-doubt. In cultivating a strong, positive attitude, you will enable your body to relax and your true potential will come through.

Self-suggestion is an excellent way to give yourself a boost of confidence a few minutes before a class or competition.

"I've been training hard and I'm prepared for this competition (class). My reflexes are sharp, my blocks are well-honed, and my footwork is evasive and explosive. My punches are powerful, and my kicks are laser-fast and can easily hit any target. I'm as good as I can be at this point in my training. I'm as good as anyone in my division (class). I'm learning from this experience and enjoying it to the utmost. I'm ready and eager for the moment."

These are general, positive suggestions that prepare your mind for your competition or class. When your subconscious mind is programmed for positive action, it will direct your body to act accordingly. You are now mentally and physically ready to compete or train at your optimum level.

Don't Program to Win

You'll notice that the above suggestions do not mention winning. It's true that as a result of developing confidence through self-suggestion you'll possess a winning attitude. However, if you were constantly to stress winning in your suggestions, your subconscious would become confused when you are scored on or lose a match in competition.

Your mind is similar to a computer. If you program it with only the suggestion to win and then you're scored on five times in a row and you lose your match, your programming is going to be disrupted and confused. What do you think that will do to your confidence?

It's far better to give yourself suggestions to perform at your best. Through your suggestions you accept the possibility you'll be scored upon and that you'll grow from the experience.

Suggest to yourself: "I'm learning from my mistakes. I know that if my opponent scores on me, I'll need to do a better job of covering my openings with my guard. If my opponent does score on me I'll remain confident and strong. I know that hitting and being hit is just part of the overall experience of sparring. I'm blocking my best, but if my opponent scores on me, I'll learn from the experience and grow as a fighter."

This is a better approach to use in your self-suggestion. With this method you can get hit but continue, having learned from the experience. Imagine how disastrous a street fight would be if you programmed yourself only to win. Getting struck might be so mentally devastating that you could easily be defeated before you had a chance to recover.

Your mind is like a computer. It can be programmed to bring out your best.

Developing a Winning Attitude

On the other hand, you can use self-suggestion to develop a winning attitude that will greatly enhance your confidence.

"I feel energy when I train and compete. I'm a winner just because I'm participating. I'm a winner because I'm gaining experience that will help me progress. I'm a winner because I'm continuously learning. Even if my opponent gets more points, I'm still a winner because I've participated and learned."

You are programming your subconscious to develop and maintain the self-image of a winner. However, the image is not based on collecting more tournament points than your opponent. You are creating a winning attitude that comes from the joy of learning, training and competing. If you happen actually to accumulate more points than the other competitors, that will enhance your positive feelings and confirm that you are on the right track in your physical training and in your mental development.

DON'T FORGET YOUR NOTEBOOK

Write these positive suggestions in your notebook after your self-suggestion session. Writing them down will help nurture in your conscious mind the seed you've planted in your subconscious. Remember, positive thoughts and goals make the best belief system because what you program into your subconscious governs how you act.

Specific Suggestions

You may give yourself suggestions that involve more specific fighting cues, such as:

"As my opponent lifts his kicking leg, I angle away from it and instantly counter with a sidekick to the knee of his support leg."

"I'm responding immediately to her hand attack with an explosive front kick to her groin."

"I'm throwing two or three backfists at my opponent's face and just as he thinks I'm going to do it again, I'll roundhouse kick his groin."

Cues such as these can be developed in your suggestions in greater detail so that your subconscious will become programmed to respond accordingly when you fight. Remember to keep your suggestions in the present tense and keep them positive. Never say, "I won't lose my balance when I sidekick." Instead say, "My balance is steady and firm as I sidekick."

PREPARING TO LEARN

It was mentioned earlier that self-suggestion prior to training or competition helps to establish confidence. It can also be used to prepare you mentally and physically for other kinds of learning.

Tai chi is a Chinese art that incorporates slow, rhythmic fighting movements that serve as an exercise, a form of moving meditation and a subtle but effective method of self-defence. Learning the forms as well as executing them requires the student's maximum concentration. I've found self-suggestion to be invaluable in my study of tai chi.

I arrive at my class about twenty minutes early so that I have extra time to prepare. I remain in my car, get into a comfortable position and induce relaxation. I then give myself suggestions as to how well I'm going to do in class.

"Tai chi is easy to learn. I'm highly receptive to learning. I'm listening to all my teacher says and I'm easily absorbing the instruction. I'm relaxed. My movements are soft. Flowing. Like a leaf blowing in the wind. This is my best class ever."

I choose suggestions that relax my body and prepare my mind to be receptive to learning. Since tai chi involves movements that are gentle and fluid, I want to be as relaxed and calm as possible. When I've reached this state, which usually takes about twenty minutes, I'm then prepared mentally and physically for the learning that follows.

I've found that this simple procedure makes a great difference in the quality of my class. On those days when I am rushing around and haven't had enough time to prepare for the class with self-suggestion, I find my mind is cluttered and my muscles want to do everything but the right thing.

SELF-SUGGESTION WHILE DRIVING?

A modified form of self-suggestion can be done while driving to class or a tournament. It's modified in the sense that you are fully awake while driving the car. The deeper form of self-suggestion, done while lying down with the eyes closed, isn't conducive to an accident-free trip.

To try this modified form of self-suggestion, first induce a pleasant sense of physical and mental relaxation through deep breathing and concentrate on relaxing your muscles. Tell yourself that although you are becoming relaxed, you are still alert and aware of your driving responsibilities. Once you are lightly relaxed (do not strive for deep relaxation), give yourself suggestions as to your class or the tournament.

This is an enjoyable and beneficial way to commute. You will arrive rested, refreshed and ready for whatever arises. You may even find you are a better driver when you are relaxed and able to react more quickly.

CAUTION: DO NOT PRACTISE SELF-SUGGESTION WHILE DRIVING IF YOU ARE AT ALL TIRED OR SLEEPY OR HAVE IN THE PAST FALLEN ASLEEP EASILY DURING A SELF-SUGGESTION SESSION.

WORDS

Here's another self-suggestion exercise that's not only easy, but fun. The process is to choose a descriptive word and translate, or act out, its definition with your actions. I call the exercise "Words."

The word I choose depends on what I want to achieve during my workout.

After I induce a mild state of relaxation, I repeat the word several times and think about its connotations. I give myself several positive suggestions to concentrate on the exercise.

Let's say I'm working on a combination and I've chosen the word "soft," which to me connotes a feeling of light, gentle, and flowing movement. I think of my movements as so soft that if someone were to touch my hand in mid-punch, my technique would be knocked off course. My arms almost wave in the air, as if they were stalks of wheat blowing gently in the wind. My kicks lift and settle back to the ground easily, without sound.

If I were practising a kata, my word might be "samurai" and I would be charged with a feeling of old Japan. I would think of myself as an actor portraying a fighting samurai in defence of some ancient mountain-top village.

If I were about to spar or shadowbox, I might choose the word "explosive." Then my techniques would define the word with artillery-like attacks, launched suddenly with great speed and tremendous power, ripping through my opponent's defences.

I choose words that present an immediate and colourful picture in my mind: *slow, smooth, explosive, quick, angry, soft, hard, powerful, samurai*. These are words I frequently use that have definite meaning to me. Your list of evocative words, and their connotations, might be different. The important thing is that your words hold a clear meaning for you, that you can translate them into specific feelings and reflect these feelings in your physical actions. A word is of no value if you just happen to like it but are unable to feel it and act it out.

Most martial arts students are unaware how self-suggestion can enhance their physical and mental training. I hope that after two or three sessions, you will discover how easy, enjoyable and beneficial it really is.

4

SWEATLESS PRACTICE

IF INDEED THERE IS A secret in the martial arts, it lies in what I call "sweatless practice." This is a simple yet highly effective tool that, although it has been around for many years, has only recently become accepted among top athletes and coaches as a viable supplement to physical training.

Sweatless practice is the act of mentally visualizing a specific physical activity, whether a single punch or kick, or the multiple movements of kata or sparring. Creating these moving pictures in the mind requires you to call up all the details of the activity—sound, colour, emotion—in their utmost clarity, from beginning to end of the sequence. The images you invoke are so vivid, so "real," that you feel as though the visualized activity has actually occurred.

The activity is sweatless because you can do it in the comfort of your easy chair. It's called practice because even though you are only visualizing it in your mind, you are receiving nearly the same benefit as if you had been physically practising the technique.

Many studies have been conducted that demonstrate the similarities between mental and physical practice. They have revealed that people who physically practise an activity and those who practise mentally show nearly the same level of improvement after a given period of time. Countless athletes, including such champions as golfer Jack Nicklaus, tennis player Chris Evert Lloyd, basketball player Bill Russell and karate great Chuck Norris, all swear by sweatless practice.

RELAX FIRST

As with self-suggestion, your mind is more receptive when you are physically and mentally relaxed. One of the best times to relax is upon awakening in the morning or just before you go to sleep at night. Since your body and mind have just rested or are preparing to rest, you are especially receptive to enhanced relaxation and visualization. However, if you find the relaxation exercises put you to sleep before you can get to your sweatless practice, you can sit up or move to a bedroom chair. Wherever you practise, it's important to keep your spine straight.

HOW TO DO IT

Let's begin with an easy practice run, visualizing a front kick.

Induce deep relaxation. Then, keeping your eyes closed, see yourself standing in your fighting stance. Picture yourself lifting your rear leg and chambering your knee near your chest. Your arms are in their on-guard position as your leg thrusts outward, until it is fully extended. Then it retracts, again chambering near your chest. Then your foot returns to the floor.

How did you do? Some people see the images as clearly and vividly as if they appeared on a TV screen, while others form only an impression or a feeling for the activity. Whichever way you visualize is fine. The important thing is that your brain experiences the activity.

Key Word

As described in Chapter 1, your key word can be used to trigger a response from the subconscious mind, in this case, an image of a specific activity. After you have practised visualization for awhile and have become comfortable with the process, you can assign a specific key word to any given practice session. Then, whenever you wish to replay a specific image, all you have to do is say the key word and the image will unfold in your mind.

It's important to place this word into your subconscious at the time you initially visualize a specific activity. After you've achieved relaxation, repeat the key word at the beginning and the end of your visualization. For example, if you're visualizing the front kick, you might say the word "front" before you perform the visualization and again at the completion of your session. This process of bracketing your session with the key word will plant the word and the image into the subconscious at the same time.

Once the key word is in place, you can call upon it anytime you want to get an instant replay of the activity. You can replay it before you go to sleep at night, before your class, or just before your tournament event. Simply induce relaxation and say your key word, and the image will unfold in your mind's eye.

Your Best Kata and Your Best Fight

Reach into your memory and retrieve your best kata performance. It may have been in your backyard, in your school or in a tournament. If it was in competition, it doesn't matter whether you placed or lost. All that's important is that you remember a particular time when all the elements of your form came together to make it the very best you've done.

After you've achieved relaxation, recreate an image in your mind's eye of your best kata performance. It's important to bring to your image every detail of the moment: the feel of your uniform; the snap of your punches; the crispness of your kicks; the speed of your techniques; the feeling of drama; the spirit of the battle; and the feeling you had knowing you had done your very best.

Put all the positiveness of that moment into your visualization. See, hear and feel it. If you received compliments after your real performance, hear them again. If you received cheers from the tournament crowd, hear those also. Recapture your best moment and replay it again and again so that it becomes embedded in your mind.

Visualize past successes to help you with future goals.

This idea can be used in other areas of your karate as well. If you've done especially well in a sparring match, you can replay that moment. Don't visualize the entire sparring session, but choose two or three scoring techniques that you consider your best. Remember everything about them: how you set them up; your stances; your timing; the precise moment of the hit; and your recovery.

Mental imagery will help you recapture special moments and increase the chance of their happening again and again. By replaying the details in your mind's eye, you program them into your subconscious, which will then guide you toward repeating those moments in the future.

Head Swapping

"Head swapping" is a mental game in which you picture yourself performing an activity in place of someone you admire. Perhaps you want to emulate your instructor's kata or another student's sidekick, back kick combination. Through the use of your imagination, you can become that person and perform your movements in the same way.

Let's try it with the combination. After you've induced relaxation, bring forth a clear mental image of your classmate. As you picture her standing in her fighting stance, superimpose your body over hers and watch as the two of you move as one person. Visualize the combination over and over again as you perform every part of the movement exactly as your classmate performs it.

If you're having trouble creating this image, try visualizing the technique as if you were seeing with your classmate's eyes. Her movements are yours but this time you are on the inside looking out, not viewing from the outside. This method will give you a different perspective as well as a feeling for the technique.

Head swapping will not give you Bill Wallace's roundhouse kick if you don't have his physical structure or his flexibility. But the mental imagery will help you progress with your own roundhouse kick within the capabilities of your own body.

Timing Is Everything

Your visualization of a physical act should take the same amount of time as the real act. If your kata takes two minutes, then your visualized kata should take two minutes. If your backfist and reverse punch combination takes one-half second to execute, then the one in your mind should take the same amount of time.

If this is difficult at first, don't give up. At first I found that a two-minute kata would take me twenty minutes to visualize. This was primarily because my ability to concentrate was poor; I continually had to bring myself back to the task at hand. With practise, however, I was able to increase my control over my thoughts. My timing eventually improved to the point that it now matches the timing of the real act.

Don't Leave Anything Out

Let's say you're visualizing three or four scoring techniques that helped you win your belt division at the last tournament. You're recalling an image of the back kick that scored and the ridgehand that broke the tie. You're visualizing the fakes and the footwork that contributed to your success.

Also, you need to remember the sounds of the crowd and the cheering of your classmates. Remember the feel of your punch as it found its way through an opponent's guard and into his abdomen. Feel the energy you had that day and let it charge your muscles. See the cheering faces. Hear your shout as your technique scores.

It's important to bring as much detail as you can to your sweatless practice. You are creating a script in your subconscious mind in which you will later play the starring role. Reach into your memory and bring to your mental movie as many sights, sounds and feelings as you can recall.

COMBINING SELF-SUGGESTION WITH SWEATLESS PRACTICE

Perhaps you've noticed that the process of sweatless practice is basically the same as that for self-suggestion. You begin in a comfortable position and then induce deep relaxation through deep breathing and selective cues. Why not take advantage of the time and combine both for a highly beneficial session?

Say you have a belt test in a week, and although you're ready physically, the idea of being examined, especially in front of other people, fills you with anxiety, nausea, weakness and inhibits your sleep.

Many people experience these symptoms before any kind of examination. There are probably as many reasons for this as there are people who are miserable with the symptoms. These feelings are all part of the "negative tapes" we discussed in Chapter 3. If you're going to progress in the fighting arts, then you need to take immediate steps to rid yourself of those tapes so that you can face those examinations with feelings of strong self-assurance. Barring any deep psychological problems, you can make this happen by combining sweatless practice with self-suggestion.

The Process

Begin as usual by inducing deep relaxation. Before you begin your suggestions, say the word "confidence." This is the key word you'll use later to fill yourself instantly with feelings of confidence.

Give yourself suggestions such as the following:

"I'm ready for this examination. My techniques are strong and fast, and my form is flawless. I've trained hard and I possess all the skills and knowledge necessary for the belt. I'm filled with knowledge that I have the ability. I'm prepared. I'm ready to face my examiners and show them I've learned their techniques. I'm walking to the centre of the room filled with confidence.

There is strength in my walk. My self-assurance radiates from my posture and from my eyes. My every move is that of a winner. I'm standing proud. My breathing is calm. I'm ready to perform."

Take your time with these suggestions. Say them slowly and pause to reflect on each one. Repeat them two or three times if you wish. When you say "there is strength in my walk," feel that strength. Feel the confidence radiating from you.

Your next step is to visualize your confidence. Say to yourself, "I'm now going to see myself confident and positive as I take my belt test. My mental images are clear and precise."

Imagine you're in your school standing calm and confident and raring to go. Your hair is combed, your uniform is washed and pressed. See yourself radiating with certainty as to your ability to perform at your best. Hear your name called and see yourself walk with a gait that virtually shouts with power and positiveness. Feel the excitement pump through your veins, supplying confident energy, strength and speed. See yourself meeting requirement after requirement with the knowledge the test has already been successfully passed. At the completion, you're standing tall and poised as the judges make the only decision they can: PASS.

At the completion of this session, say the word "confidence" to embed the key word in your subconscious before you return to your conscious state.

Tournament Preparation

Developing confidence is just one use for the self-suggestion/sweatless practice combined exercise. I've also used it as an easy way to prepare for competition.

After inducing relaxation, I tell myself how well prepared I am for the tournament and how excellent my performance is (remember always to keep your suggestions in the present tense). Then, after I've completed all my suggestions, I begin visualizing my performance.

Often my visualization serves different purposes. If I'm visualizing a new kata, I emphasize the precision of the movements to ensure that they are firmly embedded in my mind. If I'm entering an old kata at a big tournament with tough opponents, I work on enhancing my confidence so that I'm better prepared to face the tough competition. If I've grown bored with the form, I work on developing a dynamic fighting spirit.

There are many ways to incorporate self-suggestion into your sweatless practice. Whatever your need may be, give yourself powerful suggestions and then follow them up with clear and precise mental images. With practice you'll find this sweatless workout a valuable supplement to your regular training.

5

BEING THE BEST YOU CAN BE

IF YOU'RE LIKE MOST people, you probably began your karate training with the idea of beating up the school bully or developing enough confidence to walk down the street knowing you can defend yourself and your loved ones against a mean and ruthless world. These are typical goals of beginners who see the fighting arts as just fighting. But as time passes and you build a solid base of karate knowledge, you discover there is another opponent who will give you more problems than you ever imagined.

Yourself.

This opponent was there during that first class when you felt silly learning the bow; when your hands couldn't coordinate the basic punch; and when you lost your balance learning your first kick. Indeed, this opponent has been there all along—and, you can be guaranteed, will always be there.

KEEP ON FIGHTING

I began my training in the summer of 1965. I trained hard, and by the following summer I'd developed enough skill that I was able to defend myself in a couple of street encounters. I wasn't a karate expert or a superman, but I felt my training had provided me with enough skill to give me an edge against an average street fighter.

So why have I kept training to this day? Why do I continue to put myself through the pain, sweat, and injuries of vigorous karate training if I could defend myself after only a year of instruction?

The answers to these questions lie in my personal goal in karate, which is to be the very best I can be. Early in my career, I discovered my personal adversary and realized that to be my best, I had continually to fight all the human frailities that make up this formidable opponent. I had continually to spar and defeat such personality traits as fear, laziness, self-satisfaction and all the many other temptations that flesh is heir to.

I've been fighting this guy for a long time, but it's been well worth every minute of the struggle. I realize that every time I score on him there is something new I must defend against. But that's OK. Because every time I score a point, I grow a little as a person and as a martial artist.

This chapter examines your toughest opponent and just a few of the other challenges you'll face as you strive to be the best you can be. They are all typical of what the martial artist must face on the bumpy road to self-discovery. These challenges become problems only when the fighter's mind is weak and he or she confronts them negatively.

This section also contains some valuable training tips that are designed to keep your mind stimulated. When the mind is bored the body becomes stale, progress comes to a halt and regression sets in. It is important that you continually strive to stay excited about your training.

You're Not That Good

I am frequently asked by friends who do not train in the martial arts why I train so hard. "You are over forty," they say, "And you've been training since you were nineteen years old. You have a black belt in arnis and hold a master instructor rank in karate. You have lots of trophies and you've been rated as a Top Ten kata performer. So why do you keep training so hard?" The answer is simple.

I'm not that good.

How about you? Are you so good that you can now slack off and take it easy? It's good that you're good. But wouldn't it be great if you were great?

People who want to be the best they can be won't just settle for good. They have an itch to scratch, a hunger to feed, so they keep on pushing and fighting toward their ultimate best.

GET OUT OF YOUR COMFORT ZONE

An armchair athlete is a person who sits comfortably in his favourite chair and watches the game on television. His beer is cold, his chair is comfy and his team is winning. This person has entered a place far worse than the Twilight Zone. Indeed, he's just slipped into that nearly inescapable place called THE COMFORT ZONE.

It's Hard to Escape

Although the name of the place doesn't sound so terrible, be on guard against falling into its warm, inviting arms. Once there, you'll never progress because you'll never get out of your chair and away from the television. It's always easiest to maintain the status quos; pushing onward and upward takes hard work. Your natural tendency is to seek out and accept what is easiest and most comfortable. Your progress in the fighting arts depends on how well you can fight this inviting temptation.

Once you get into the comfort zone and begin skipping workouts, it's hard to get out.

Now if your body really requires rest ("really" is the key word here), then by all means enjoy relaxation and extra sleep. But be careful! It's easy to get fooled and convince yourself to skip your workout for some extra rest, since it's more comfortable than getting sweaty, tired and punched.

To be your best, you must pull yourself out of your comfort zone and into a disposition favourable to learning and progressing. You will soon see the results of your effort. By going faithfully to class you will learn new techniques, improve old ones, strengthen your body, and develop your reflexes and all the mental skills that are vital to your art. But if you sink back into your comfort zone, content with past achievements, you'll make no progress at all. In fact, you may even regress.

Sometimes, putting in the extra training required for forms competition can be tough. I find those last three weeks before a tournament to be gruelling, especially when I would rather be reading a novel or watching a movie. That lazy part of me is always there, hovering over my shoulder, offering me all the riches of my sofa, potato chips and a soda. "You know the form already," it whispers in its weary, sluggish voice. "Besides, what do you need with another trophy? Take it easy, relax and get comfortable."

Although at times this argument can seem convincing, I always remind myself that competing at my very best is what I want to do. I want to compete better than I did last time. I want to progress, not maintain what I've already achieved. I also know it can be lonely out in the middle of the kata ring. When I'm out there the audience and the judges are witnessing the product of my preparation, all the effort I've put into reaching this moment. They don't care how much training I've avoided or how many movies I've seen. As I walk out to compete, they're concerned only with my skill.

That reminder always gets me up out of my chair to put in that extra training time.

Only you can decide where you want to be. Are you going to settle into that comfort zone where everything is easy because nothing is happening? Are you going to be an armchair martial artist? Or are you going to be a person who knows that to move ahead requires extra effort, an extra bit of intestinal fortitude that will eventually pay off?

THE TRAINING HABIT

Not training can become easy. You skip one workout and that lazy part of your brain wakes up just long enough to say, "Hey, that was easy. I'm going to do that again." You skip another and another and soon you're skipping one or two workouts a week. Before you know it, a habit has developed. By having regularly skipped workouts, you've established a pattern, an automatic response to your slightest hesitation or excuse not to train.

To be the best you can be, you need to rid yourself of negative habits and replace them with positive ones. You must firmly inplant in your mind that missed workouts won't do anything for your progress and that missed training is time lost forever. You should feel a sense of guilt about the missed class, a valuable block of time you'll never again have the opportunity to experience.

You're given only so much time on earth. If you've chosen to make the martial arts part of your life, then you need to allot a certain amount of time for this activity. However, if you choose to replace that time with, say, TV watching, you've cheated your goal, your art, and yourself.

A program I've found helpful over the years is my habit of doing something toward my art every day. No, I don't train physically every day, nor do I recommend that you should. The body needs to rest. However, I program myself to do something each day so that my mind stays disciplined and my goal stays alive. My own program is as follows:

Monday	Class	2 hours
Tuesday	Read/Write/Train	1 hour
Wednesday	Class	2 hours
Thursday	Read/Write/Train	1 hour
Friday	Class	2 hours
Saturday	Read/Write/Train	1 hour
Sunday	Read/Write	1 hour

On Monday, Wednesday and Friday, I teach and train in my school. On Tuesday, Thursday and Saturday, I have a choice of three things I can do, depending on my needs. For example, if I'm working on a martial arts article, I write. If I just want to relax, I'll read a martial arts magazine or book. But if I have an abundance of energy or an upcoming tournament, I'll train.

Although my class time is precise, 6:30 to 8:30, the other days are less structured. Sometimes my efforts will take more than an hour and sometimes less. Occasionally I'll combine two things, such as writing for three hours and training for thirty minutes. One day I might read a magazine for fifteen minutes, while on another day I might go for a marathon solo workout. Sunday I do a little reading and writing and encourage myself to rest and store up energy for the next week.

My mind has accepted this pattern and it has become a positive habit. This program keeps me disciplined and focused on my goal, yet leaves plenty of time for family, friends and fishing. I've not gone overboard and become exclusively focused on the martial arts.

This positive training habit has become so ingrained in my mind that, on those rare days when some unexpected event prevents me from working on my art, I feel profoundly that I have lost something vital to me. It's as if I had skipped a meal and were now hungry. Even when the missed training was unavoidable, I experience a feeling of emptiness and guilt.

Develop your own habit-forming program. If you can make time for eating and sleeping, you can make time for your art. Your mind will quickly condition itself to the schedule and you'll be surprised how easy it is not to skip a workout.

SACRIFICING

We are a spoiled society, used to having the microwave turn out a hot breakfast in two minutes, able to watch a major motion picture on a video cassette in the comfort of our living room, and able to fly anywhere in the world in a matter of hours. If we have the cash, or a charge card, we can possess just about anything our hearts desire.

Except skill in the martial arts.

Of course you can buy lessons, but actual skill in the fighting arts costs much more than money. Skill is something you acquire only after you recognize that it isn't just another credit card transaction. Skill becomes yours once you've spent millions in sweat, sacrifice and discipline.

Striving to be your best means you'll have to sacrifice things that are pleasurable. There will be times when your training schedule will interfere with your going to a party; a tournament will fall on the same day as a picnic; and maintaining your fighting weight will mean foregoing an extra piece of pie à la mode. Sacrifice means having to give up some short-term pleasures for the long-lasting benefits you get from your training.

Friday Night Training

I offer a one-hour, Friday evening class from 6:30 to 7:30. Although the other weeknight classes are two hours long, the Friday class is purposely only an hour so that students can get in a workout and can still go out for the evening. Still, Friday's class has the fewest number of students. Instead of working out and taking in a movie later in the evening or arranging to arrive at their party a little late, many students choose to skip the training altogether.

It's not at all surprising that those people who consistently train on Friday are my best students. Although the fact that they are good karate students cannot be attributed solely to their Friday night attendance, it indicates some of the sacrifices they are making to be the best they can be.

Fighting Temptation

It's not always easy to say no to the many temptations that arise. A couple of beers with friends sounds more inviting than an hour of getting punched and kicked. However, once you've set a powerful goal for yourself you'll have strength to resist. When you've practised self-suggestion, positive imagery and all the skills discussed in this book, your mind and heart will be set. Then, when you're confronted with all the delights of instant pleasure, you'll clearly recognize that they must not interfere with your karate. You'll easily say no to them or arrange alternative times for them.

After a while you'll not even view this discipline as a sacrifice. Pleasures you thought were going to be hard to give up will no longer be important and, as a result, passing them by will not seem a hardship. Your goal of being the best you can be will far overshadow these momentary pleasures.

Why Me?

While striving to be your best, you must accept some of life's cruel little jokes. It often seems as though, every time you get ahead, you run smack into an obstacle. As the old saying goes, "Every time I take one step forward, I get knocked back two."

One of my advanced students recently lamented, "Whenever I decide to concentrate on my sparring and begin to make progress, I jam a finger or sprain a toe. It never fails. And about a week before a tournament, I always strain an old injury on the back of my right leg. As regular as clockwork, it flares up and threatens to sideline me from competition." Although he never misses a competition, his leg is one of those obstacles that distracts his attention and makes the going a little harder than he would like.

The Path

The course of study that a martial artist chooses is called "the way" or "the path." Not only is it a rocky path—it has boulders, deep holes and even pits filled with man-eating alligators. I'm not warning you to deter you from taking the path, but to prepare you for the journey. To reach for your best, you must be willing to accept these obstacles, large or small, and not let them discourage or hold you back. You must face them head on, defeat them and grow stronger.

Held Back Because of a Finger

There are students who jam a finger and then stay home until the injury completely heals. This is a waste of time! When eventually the student returns, if he ever does, he'll be out of shape and will have fallen behind in the class. All the time he stayed home to watch his finger heal is time lost.

What would this person do if he hurt his finger while fighting for his life—ask the attacker to stop for a few days so his injury will heal? Of course not. He would use his other hand and both feet to keep on fighting. And that's exactly what he should do in his training.

Grow Stronger from Your Injuries

Whenever I injure a finger I don't look at it as a setback. It's disappointing, of course, but I'll just use the healing time to work on my kicks. I'll hold my injured hand behind my back, hook my fingers in my belt and work on drills and sparring with my remaining weapons.

If I've injured a toe or badly bruised a shin, I'll work primarily on my hand techniques and do a lot of leg stretching, doubling the amount of time I usually spend on my flexibility exercises. As a result, I always recuperate from injuries and come back as strong as, if not stronger than, before.

It doesn't do any good to complain and say "Why me?" Your energy is better spent making these inevitable obstacles a positive experience. To be the best you can be, you must accept that there will be obstacles along your path and that they will present themselves at the most inopportune times. But with acceptance and a positive outlook, you'll be able to face them, defeat them and grow stronger from the experience.

A Comeback Story

In 1983 I decided to enter kata competition after staying away from tournaments for eight years. Although I'd made the decision to return to the tournament arena, I felt there were three strikes against me. I was thirty-seven years old, I had an old knee injury that had plagued me for several years, and I'd been out of competition for a long time. Individually, these were not insurmountable problems, but compounded together they made a formidable obstacle to overcome. I was sitting around brooding about this when it occurred to me that this kind of thinking was detrimental. If I were serious about succeeding, I needed a plan of action, some immediate goals and a positive approach to my situation.

If you injure your hand, use your other one and your feet. Don't let an obstacle stop you; work around it and grow stronger from the experience.

My first goal was modest: to increase my training intensity in order to raise my skill to a level where I wouldn't embarrass myself in front of hundreds of people. Although I'd been practising my katas regularly, black belt competition requires long, hard preparation. But I was ready to do what was necessary. I'd created a goal and I was now hungry to satisfy it.

I trained arduously. Within three months I felt I'd gotten into good shape and my kata was tournament-ready. I felt pretty good. I'd reached the first step of my goal. Now for the next one: to enter a tournament.

As I warmed up along the sidelines, I was filled with dread and excitement. The butterflies were going berserk in my stomach and my mind was asking over and over, "Why am I doing this to myself?" People who swim the English Channel probably ask themselves the same question just before they make their dive. But I was there and committed; this was not the time to get philosophical.

Out of twenty competitors, I took fourth place. It was tough competition and I had to play off a tie to win the twelve-inch, red-and-gold trophy. I felt good about that win. In fact, to this day it remains my favourite, because it represents my win over fear, age and physical weakness.

Sometimes the small trophies have greater meaning than the large ones.

I took a few days to enjoy my accomplishments. I thought about retiring from competition again, but then I started wondering if my win was just a fluke. So I set another goal: to compete in order to determine whether I was really competition material.

In the next tournament I won a second place, the time after that third place and, at one of the largest tournaments in North America, I captured a first-place win. I felt pretty good after that and again thought about retiring, since I really had nothing to prove.

But after a couple of months I got hungry again and decided I needed to set new goals to avoid stagnating. My goal now was to be rated in *Karate Illustrated* magazine's Region 1 as a Top Ten kata competitor. This meant I had to train hard, compete frequently and win often in order to accumulate the necessary points to be rated over all the other competitors trying to do the same thing.

My hunger for this goal provided the necessary energy to train and enter tournament after tournament. By my thirty-ninth birthday my name appeared in the ratings. I was thrilled over this accomplishment because I'd success-fully conquered many obstacles, especially my knee injury.

Nine years earlier, after surgery on my left knee, the doctors told me I would always walk with a limp, probably need to use a cane and certainly never practise karate again. That was a hard diagnosis to compete against. But with a positive attitude and continual reevaluation of my goals, I proved the doctors wrong.

Awards: Plastic And Otherwise

Although I value winning, I'm not a trophy hound interested only in filling my den with ornate pieces of plastic. Sure, it's fun winning a trophy because it's a tangible sign from your peers that they consider you've done well. But my overall goal is to try and improve myself continually. Even when I'm defeated, I feel good knowing I did my best and have improved from my last effort.

My next goal is to do well in my forties. I want to keep myself in shape, stay healthy and train and compete as hard as I can.

Whatever happens, I know I can't stop now.

EXTRA EFFORT

In my school the belt ranking progresses from white to yellow, blue, blue second class, green, green second class, brown third class, brown second class, brown first class and black. On the average, a green belt takes about a year and a half to earn. Although green is halfway through the belt system, it's actually about one-third of the way to the coveted black belt because of the extra time and effort required to progress through the remaining succes-sion of belts.

A student of average physical and mental abilities can reach green belt in a year and a half by attending class three times a week, while the above-aver-age student can possibly make it in the same time by attending only twice weekly. At the green belt level, the student has acquired fast and powerful karate basics and a good working knowledge of jujitsu and arnis. It's a level where the foundation is strong and where complex skills begin to develop. Therein lies the rub.

Interestingly, in most schools this middle point, whether it's symbolized by a green belt or some other colour, is a place where a large number of students drop out. Some students are willing to put in the extra training effort to progress past this point while others are not. It's usually a time of stagnation, a plateau where only extra effort will get the student out. Students become discouraged if they are not willing to put in the extra effort or have not yet realized that their old training schedule will no longer suffice.

Get Hungry

If you have a desire to achieve your very best, you must be willing to put in the extra effort to get there. Perhaps you've reached green belt or a comparable rank. You should feel good about your achievement because few people make it that far. But now you need to get hungry to move on, and be willing to do whatever it takes to progress. You need to push yourself mentally and physically to reach even greater heights.

Talk to your instructor and ask what you need to do to get moving again. Use your own creative skills to take what you already know and to develop new exercises, drills and fighting techniques. At this point in your training, you have a large amount of knowledge upon which to draw and create. Most people know more than they think they do. If you know fifty techniques, you'll know a thousand when you start putting them into combinations and adding various types of footwork.

Try to train with a brown belt or ask your instructor if you can practise with the brown belt class. This will not only benefit you physically but will tease you mentally, by stirring your desire to progress to brown belt.

Use sweatless practice and self-suggestion to program your mind toward progress. If your immediate goal is earning your next belt, then concentrate your efforts in that direction. Remember, your actions will follow your intentions. Therefore, keep your thoughts positive and directed forward.

Do not be satisfied with where you are. If you've come this far (remember how clumsy and awkward you were in the beginning?), think how much farther you can go. Now is not the time to be complacent; in fact, there is never a time for complacency.

An old Chinese proverb says, "A journey of a thousand miles begins with a single step." If you've already traveled five hundred or even a thousand miles, don't stop now. Dig down deep and pull out that extra effort. You'll never know how far you can travel unless you keep on stepping.

Don't Stop Now

The black belt and the skill it represents is a lofty goal for anyone in the martial arts. Earning this high rank requires hard work, a lot of time, discipline and dedication. How ironic then, that after so much hard work, many black belts give up training hard or quit training altogether, thinking they've reached the end! The reason for this falling away is usually that they have not set proper goals. They've made the mistake of setting a mere length of black cloth as their ultimate and final goal, rather than seeing it simply as a mark of achievement along their path of learning.

All too often people are content to rest on just one achievement. They work hard to develop a flying side kick, or win a tournament, or earn a black belt. Then after reaching that goal, they lie back and relax in their self-satisfaction. Feeling good about your accomplishment is fine, but to stop progressing after you've gone only so far is a terrible waste of your potential.

Reaching a goal demonstrates that you have the physical and mental skills necessary to advance. But if you think you no longer have to train because you've reached the top (how many "masters" teach but never train?), you're apt to be disappointed when you find those hard-earned skills beginning to dissipate. In time, often a very short time, you find you can no longer do even those basics you needed to reach your early goals. That's called REGRESSION.

To be the best you can be, you can't rest on your laurels after reaching one goal or even ten. Striving for your best means you are always reaching, never being satisfied with past achievements. You may pause now and then to celebrate a job well done, but then you quickly move on.

You want to take advantage of your forward momentum and use its energy to keep you enthusiastic and hungry for more. Work to create a positive cycle that keeps spinning and nurturing itself.

6

FEAR

THERE ARE TWO TYPES of threat: real and imagined. Fear in the face of real threat is a positive response and may actually heighten your ability to perform. In a dangerous situation, such as being confronted by a mugger, the human body instinctively undergoes physiological changes that prepare it for battle or flight. The breathing becomes more rapid and a surge of adrenalin pours into the bloodstream. The pulse and blood pressure increase as additional blood flows to the arms and legs. The tissues receive more fuel from the liver and the vision becomes sharper.

Fear arising from an imagined threat, however, is a negative response that can impede your performance because it distorts reality. When fear and the imagination join, an average-size tournament opponent will take on the appearance of a monster, with huge, hairy hands and feet capable of reducing you to a whimpering, smouldering heap.

As your sense of danger increases, your confidence diminishes and you become helpless. You feel you're physically incompetent because your imagination has you convinced that your opponent will most assuredly end your life. This kind of fear will make you short of breath; you will lack energy and your muscles will feel stiff and heavy. As a result, your reflexes will be slow to react and your movements will lack smoothness.

Negative fear feeds on itself, creating a never-ending cycle. All of the undesirable physical reactions will affect your performance, with the result that your opponent will easily be able to score on you. This will reinforce your feeling of vulnerability and incompetence, which in turn will continue to weaken your performance.

42

As this cycle continues, your perceptions and beliefs will become increasingly distorted. You'll begin to lack confidence whenever you spar. Soon thereafter, you'll begin to doubt your abilities as a martial artist. Eventually, you may even develop a distorted opinion about yourself as a person. Obviously, if you're going to have a future in karate and grow as a person, you must confront this fear and deal with it positively.

ANALYZING YOUR FEAR

Three factors contribute to fear. First, a feeling of danger tells you that a specific threat can cause you harm. Secondly, you experience a feeling of vulnerability and, thirdly, you believe you are incapable of contending with the danger. Examine one of your fears and you will see that these three factors are all present.

To educate yourself about your fear, you need to analyze every specific facet so that you understand it completely. Since we usually generalize our feelings, breaking the fear down is a good way to begin. For example, when you say you're afraid of a certain student in your class, that's a general statement that needs to be broken down in order to analyze why and under what circumstances the fear manifests itself. You would begin by asking yourself questions such as the following:

- Am I afraid of him before class begins?
- Am I afraid of him while the class is practising kata?
- Am I afraid of him while we're working on drills?
- Am I afraid of him while we practise self-defence?
- Am I afraid of him while we spar?

Let's say you've determined you're afraid of this person when you spar. Let's break this discovery down even further by asking more questions.

- Am I afraid because he's an advanced student?
- Am I afraid because he has poor control of his techniques?
- Am I afraid I'll look bad in front of the other students?
- Am I afraid to discover I'm not as good as I think I am?

If after analyzing this list, you conclude that each item contributes to your fear, then you need to put them in order of importance. They are now statements.

1. I'm afraid because he's an advanced student.
2. I'm afraid I'll look inferior to him.
3. I'm afraid I'll look bad in front of the class.
4. I'm afraid because he has poor control.
5. I'm afraid to learn that I'm not as good as I think I am.

With this list you'll then examine each fear to determine which is real and which is imagined. Remember, the primary difference between negative fear and positive fear is that the former is based on illusion and the latter on reality. Let's choose number (4) and examine it by asking the very worst that could happen.

Could I get killed?

It's a remote possibility, but no one has been killed in my school and I haven't heard of accidental karate deaths anywhere else.

Could I get crippled for life?

Again, it's possible but the chance is remote. No one has ever been crippled in my school, nor have I heard of anyone being permanently crippled at other schools.

Could I get hurt just a little?

Sure. That happens frequently, in class and in tournaments. The injury usually takes the form of a cut lip, jammed toe or a sprained finger. Since these minor injuries are a reality, you next ask:

Can I live with these injuries and accept them as part of my karate training?

Of course. You've been hurt before and you'll probably get hurt again. After all, you're studying karate, not flower arranging.

This was a simple process of analyzing a fear. By breaking it down and asking a few questions, the imagined fear is destroyed and you're able to see the situation more realistically.

Let's take a look at item (1), "I'm afraid because he's an advanced student." Say you're a green belt with about two years of training and he's a black belt with about eight years. The fact that he has been training several years longer than you cannot be argued. But is this fact a reason to fear him? Let's use the question-and-answer format again to analyze the problem.

Are you afraid of the black cotton belt?

No, not in the literal sense of the question. Unless, of course, he were to take it off and strangle me with it.

Are you afraid of the man?

Yes. He has black belt punches and kicks and he can score on me.

What happens if he scores on you with those black belt techniques?

Well . . . nothing. It's to be expected. He's a black belt.

Does it hurt when he scores on you?

Sometimes a technique lands a little hard, and it will hurt.

What do you do then?

Nothing. I just keep sparring.

If you're not overly concerned about getting hit hard and you've accepted the idea he's a black belt and will be able to socre on you, where's the problem?

Well . . .

When he scores on you, can you stop and ask how he did it?

Oh, yes; he's very helpful.

Would you learn something from what he tells you?

Yes, I guess I would.

You're not bothered when he scores on you, you've accepted an occasional hard blow as part of the game and you've just said you would learn from the experience. So what the heck are you afraid of?

Well . . . I guess I don't remember.

Breaking your fears down and analyzing them is one approach to gaining a greater understanding of the problem. Although the above question-and-answer technique is brief, you can see how the process can reduce the opponent from an imaginary fierce monster, to a human being with advanced karate skills. You'll then be able to train with him, respecting his skills and experience, without being hampered by an unrealistic fear.

Breaking down and analyzing your fear will enable you to see even your most formidable opponent as just an opponent with advanced skills and experience.

DESENSITIZING YOUR FEAR THROUGH ACTION

Through the process of desensitizing, you face your fear directly, although in gradual stages. Gordon Liddy, one of Richard Nixon's Watergate conspirators, wrote in his book, *Will,* that as a boy he had an intense fear of rats. Liddy, an individual who brings unique solutions to problems, conquered his fear through culinary means. He forced himself to face the very thing he feared most. He captured a large rat, killed it, and lightly cooked it over a small fire. Then he ate it.

Of course I'm not suggesting that you capture, kill, cook and eat the black belt who has been causing you anxiety. However, it is important that you confront your fear and deal with it in a positive and beneficial manner.

The only way to defeat fear is to face it head on. One way might be to set a goal of sparring with this black belt. Although this could be approached all at once by simply gritting your teeth and challenging him to a match, there's too great a chance of the outcome affecting you even more negatively. A better approach would be to work toward your goal gradually. This way you're building a sound foundation of confidence that will provide you with support so that you can eventually spar with him and enjoy the experience.

The first stage is just to talk with him. If you've not formally met, take a moment before class to introduce yourself and tell him you've admired his skill for a long time. Tell him how much you enjoyed his fighting in the last tournament. Nothing breaks the ice like a compliment. With that out of the way, you'll find it much easier to approach him in the future.

The next time you see him, ask his advice on developing a good round-house kick, since you consider his to be one of the best you've seen. Show him your kick and ask if there is anything you could be doing differently.

By approaching him in this manner, you're desensitizing yourself to any unrealistic and distorted fears you may have created in your mind. Monsters don't talk and smile and demonstrate their techniques. Monsters kill their prey. Since you haven't been killed, he must not be a monster. You're also learning something from him. The very source of your fear is actually helping you to learn karate. Monsters won't help you. Nice people help you. Therefore, he must be a nice person.

The next stage is to inquire about his ideas regarding sparring. How does he employ such tactics as timing, broken rhythm, faking and counter-attacking? When he demonstrates his techniques, you'll have passed another barrier, the fear of his punching and kicking at you. You're on the receiving end of his punches and kicks, but the situation is controlled and limited. Again, you've survived and learned something.

Once you feel you've laid a solid foundation of confidence, ask to slow spar with him. This is your opportunity to experiment with various attacks and counters while your distorted and unrealistic fears dissolve. Sure, he'll score on you but you'll survive. By having approached this moment in gradual, confidence-building stages, you've systematically chipped away at the distortions created by your imagination. As a result, you can now inter-react with the object of your fear.

Fast sparring is the final stage, although after what has gone before, this should feel anticlimactic. The fear you have now is a nervous fear based on what is real rather than what has been falsely created in the mind. The black belt fighter is strong and fast and will probably score on you most of the time. But having desensitized yourself gradually, you realize he is not the monstrous killer you imagined.

The Final Cleansing

After your sparring session, tell him of your original fears. Explain that you once had a phobia about fighting him, but because of his kind help, you've dissolved the barrier. Expressing this aloud to him is a way of finally defeating your obstacle and imprinting a positive and convincing statement on your mind.

Having the courage to fight the black belt does not demonstrate a lack of fear. Instead, you've demonstrated your acceptance of the fact that in order to conquer unrealistic fear, you must face it. You must strip away the delusions and use the positive fear as energy. Remember: if you don't overcome it, fear will control you and stifle your growth.

SELF-SUGGESTION AND MENTAL IMAGERY TO CONQUER FEAR

(See Chapters 4 and 5 for additional ways to quiet the imagination and develop a realistic view of fear.)

WISE FIGHTERS KNOW THEIR LIMITATIONS

You can apply all these principles and you'll probably still be afraid to fight an attacker who is armed with a chainsaw. The ability to determine whether a threat is real or imagined should keep you from wading into a situation beyond your capabilities. By analyzing the situation and understanding your skills and weaknesses, you'll have more information on which to base your decisions.

Ask yourself whether attempting this confrontation is reasonable for you at this stage in your development. I would certainly fear an assailant with a chainsaw, and I know my fear is based on reality—he could hack me to bits. But facing my fear doesn't mean I would walk into a confrontation with him. More likely I would turn around and run like the wind.

7

MUSHIN:
THE MIND OF NO MIND

THE FIGHT

THE KARATE MASTER made a seemingly casual observation of the five men encircling him. His mind remained calm as his eyes gathered in the details: five men, one armed with a knife; one well over six feet tall, 220 pounds; one very intoxicated; one nervous and one barking orders to the others.

The master remained sedate, his heart rate and breathing elevated only slightly, his eyes remote, almost as if he were looking in the distance. He slowly turned 360 degrees. His face held no emotion and his mind was clear as he perceived everything around him. The 220-pounder charged first.

Like a whirlwind, the master's body spun, and his foot smashed into the man's cheekbone. Even before the first man fell, the knife fighter leaped forward with the blade but instantly found his arm caught in a painful jujitsu hold. His screams blended with the sickening snap of his elbow joint.

As the master spun away, his powerful side kick impaled the intoxicated attacker's abdomen, sending him to the ground, gasping for air. The ringleader shouted for the remaining man to attack, but the master's piercing gaze and calm, relaxed posture held the frightened man back. After a moment, the would-be attacker fled.

The master stood quietly, observing the three fallen men and the one who remained standing, the leader. The master waited, his mind clear, aware of everything, lingering on nothing as it flowed without obstruction. His thoughts did not dwell on what he had just done, nor was he planning his future actions. His mind was like a lake without ripples. It only reflected.

Just as the ringleader started to move toward the master, he was distracted by the barking hacks of the intoxicated man, who for a moment considered getting up but then changed his mind. The ringleader's eyes darted nervously from the master to the fallen three and then back to the master. A brief moment of decision passed before he turned and ran in the direction of the coward.

Many of today's fighting arts were adapted from observing the fighting and survival characteristics of various animals and insects. Shaolin monks purportedly studied every move of such creatures as the preying mantis, white crane, monkey and tiger, from which they subsequently named their systems of fighting.

For years these monks worked to emulate the fluidity, speed and explosiveness of these creatures. Yet a problem arose, rooted in the one thing that makes humans unique and superior to all the other creatures of the earth: the ability to reason.

The monks discovered that since they were human, they had the ability to plot attacks and counter-attacks, which would cause them to fix their minds on a single aspect of their opponent to the exclusion of other information. This fixation of the mind would then leave them vulnerable to a surprise attack. Since this could prove fatal, they strove to devise ways to empty the mind of preconceptions.

TAKUAN

The Japanese word for a clear, empty mind is *mushin* (pronounced moo-shin). Literally translated as no-mind, or non-abiding mind, mushin can be traced back several hundred years to the times of the great Zen master and swordsman, Takuan. This great swordsman is believed to have been one of the first to apply Zen, specifically the concept of mushin, to the art of fighting with a sword. Although this blending was initially between Zen and swordsmanship, mushin can be applied to all fighting arts.

Takuan wrote:

To speak in terms of your military art, if you see in a glance your opponent's striking sword and think, I'll block him there, your mind will get stuck on your opponent's sword, the motion will go out of your swordplay and you will be cut down.

FIGHTING MULTIPLE ATTACKERS

The karate master at the beginning of this chaper was surrounded by five people, all possessing dangerous characteristics. One attacker was large and powerful, another was armed with a knife, while a third man's courage was fortified with alcohol. It was important to notice the presence of a ringleader and that the group had a possible weak link, a frightened man, although he might be the most dangerous.

If you were to ask five different martial artists how they would defend themselves in this situation, you would probably get five different responses. One fighter might say it's best to concentrate on the knife, since it has the deadliest potential. Another might argue that to attack the biggest and strongest assailant would have a weakening psychological effect on the group. A third fighter would favour taking out the ringleader to weaken the other four. Indeed, there are a number of possibilities.

The karate master, however, did not need to analyze the situation. A quick glance at the danger encircling him was enough for his brain to register the five individuals and their specific characteristics. He didn't ponder any one in particular. He kept his eyes open and his mind clear of preconceived thoughts of attack and defence. His mind flowed and was not encumbered by such thoughts as KNIFE! or RINGLEADER! and thus he was able to react to the demands of the moment.

Takuan wrote:

> . . . *even if ten men with swords came at you all at once, if you deal with but one man and not dwell on what happens afterwards, you won't miss a move. The mind moves in response to the ten men ten times, and if the mind does not dwell on any one of them, you will move and confront them one after another and there will be no trace of inadequacy. However, if you stop the mind and face only one man, you may be able to deal with him, but you will surely fail with the next man.*

THE FLOWING MIND

The mushin mind flows continuously, grasping at nothing, holding onto nothing. The mind moves naturally, unconsciously, flowing like water and filling every possible corner. The karate master fought only what was presented to him at a specific moment. His mind flowed freely as he dealt with one assailant after another.

A fighter whose mind isn't clear and flowing, but is cluttered with thoughts of being hit by the 220-pound man or stabbed by the armed man, will have trouble reacting spontaneously. As soon as his mind locks in on the knife, the intoxicated man could strike him from behind. As soon as the fighter dwells on poking the ringleader in the eyes, the coward could easily kick him in the groin. When the mind fixes on one thing, it is not free to react to another.

"If you look at your opponent's sword you will be killed by it," runs an old saying. In other words, if your concentration is so focused on your opponent's weapon, whether a fist, foot or knife, you'll be unable to see all of his potential as well as the surroundings. This problem is sometimes called "tunnel vision" because it's like looking through a tunnel and seeing only a small spot of light at the other end. There may be great beasts on either side of that small circle, but you see only the light.

The mushin mind flows unencumbered, aware of everything, but not focusing on any one thing.

THE CLOSED MIND

Karate fighters can easily fall prey to their own preconceptions when sparring. Let's say you're sparring with Susan, who possesses a fast and powerful roundhouse kick. Knowing this, you're anticipating the kick and have a plan of sidestepping it, blocking and then countering with a hard punch to her abdomen. As you begin sparring, you're waiting and watching for the kick. You're shuffling around, anxious to slam home your counter-punch. Suddenly, she leaps forward with a mighty shout and whips a powerful ridgehand strike next to your ear. OK, so she caught you off guard. You move around again, ready for her famous roundhouse, but again you get tagged—this time with a backfist. This pattern will continue because your mind is not open and free to perceive a variety of possibilities. As a result of fixing on one thing, your mind has become closed to everything else.

Let's examine this problem under slightly different circumstances. This time it's you who possess a devastating technique, a backfist you're anxious to show everyone watching, especially your opponent.

You stalk your opponent, planning how your backfist will tear through the air and smack solidly next to her ear. The reality, however, is that the more you dwell on delivering your one technique, the easier it is for your opponent to hit you. By letting your mind become preoccupied with one idea, you've lost your freedom to act and react.

Can You Remove a Thought?

To acquire mushin might seem difficult, since trying to remove one thought from the mind usually just replaces it with another. Then when you try to remove the second thought, you'll replace it with a third—and so on. An ancient poem written by a perplexed lover expresses a similar dilemma:

To think that I am not going
To think of you anymore
Is still thinking of you
Let me then try not to think
That I am not going to think of you

The more you try to catch a butterfly, the more it flutters just out of reach. But if you sit very still, it may come softly and sit on your shoulder. The harder you try to achieve mushin, the more difficult it will be to attain. When it does happen, however, it will be a wonderful surprise because it happens when you are least expecting it. Suddenly, you'll attack or defend without having given the moment any previous thought. It will happen so spontaneously that you will probably be more surprised than even your opponent.

DEVELOPING THE MUSHIN MIND

There are a few exercises that you can include in your regular training to help you move toward mushin. It's important to remember, however, that you not dwell on trying to achieve mushin. Work on these exercises and soon, when you least expect it, mushin will arise.

Gazing

There is a concept in kendo training called "fixing one's eyes on the far mountains."
Takuan wrote:

Fixing one's eyes on the far mountains means to gaze far and wide. One exercise practised by samurai is to look at all far away things as if they were close and all close things as if they were far away. In this way, the entire field of any situation is surveyed as though one were looking at mountains in the distance.

Try using your opponent's solar plexus as your primary focal point. Don't just look at him, but gaze as if you were seeing through the solar plexus off into the distance. Never concentrate, or allow your eyes to focus on any one thing; be aware of your opponent in his totality. From this centre point, you can easily see the rest of him in your peripheral vision.

Gaze through your opponent's solar plexus as you await his attack or an opening in his defence. When an opening does occur, hit, or when you are attacked, block. Give the moment only limited attention and then immediately let your mind clear and be ready for whatever happens next.

It's paramount that you do not react to an opening by thinking, "Oh boy, an opening! I think I'll sidekick it with my left foot." Or when you are attacked say, "Uh-oh, here comes a kick! I think I'll sidestep and block it with my lead hand then . . ."

In both instances your mind has lingered and become fixed while you make your decision. Meanwhile, the opening disappears and your opponent's kick finds its mark.

A Fixed Mind Is Easily Fooled

When the mind has becomed fixed, it is susceptible to being fooled. When all your thoughts are focused on your opponent's backfist, she can easily slip in a reverse punch. This is what makes a fake effective (see Chapter 9).

When your mind is clear and free of anticipation, you'll respond only to your opponent's initial movement and then continue to flow as your mind monitors input. For example, when your opponent launches a backfist fake, your brain will immediately acknowledge the movement, send a defensive response and then continue to flow. You'll give the moment only enough attention to block, duck or ignore the movement, then your mind will instantly clear and be aware of any follow-up attacks. You will not be easily fooled because your mind has not stopped on the fake. You will be aware of it only as long as it exists, a very short duration. Since the real attack usually follows the fake, the mushin mind has a much greater chance of perceiving it.

Two-Person Mushin Reaction Drill

I like to use this drill in my class to help my students experience the mushin mind. The class forms two lines, one facing the other, in their fighting stances. The goal, one that's crucial and makes the difference whether or not the students experience mushin, is to strive for maximum physical and mental relaxation. It's imperative that their minds are totally calm and void of any anticipation of what will take place. Frequently, I'll prepare them for the exercise by talking them through one of the relaxation exercises in Chapter 1. To relax them further and alleviate any concern over winning and losing, I stress there is to be no competition.

The exercise is set up with partners taking turns attacking and defending. For example, Bob and Susan assume their stances and gaze calmly at each other's solar plexus. Bob launches a slow backfist and, since Susan's mind is clear, she perceives the backfist and immediately blocks. The moment her block makes contact with his attacking arm, her mind clears and is flowing, ready for whatever happens next.

Now it's Susan's turn. She throws a slow punch to Bob's midsection. The image of the punch enters Bob's unobstructed mind and he easily responds appropriately, then allows his mind to clear and continue to flow freely. Bob and Susan continue this exchange, using a variety of offensive and defensive techniques.

Although they will eventually increase their speed, it's important that they do not speed up too soon. It's far more important for the development of mushin that the students learn to control their minds and bodies. If they practise with speed before they are mentally ready, then the drill is no different from any other and mushin does not arise.

The first time I taught this drill, I was amazed how quickly those students with only a few months of training caught on. The students were impressed with how effectively they responded to random attacks, as long as they kept their minds unencumbered. On the other hand, they discovered that they could not block as well when they became distracted. If they looked at another classmate, allowed their minds to wander, or tried to anticipate their opponent's techniques, they did not experience mushin.

Three-Person Mushin Reaction Drill

After a few practice sessions with the Two-Person Mushin Reaction Drill, the students break into groups of three, with one person designated as the defender. Again, it's important that everyone is physically and mentally relaxed to maximize the effectiveness of the drill.

Once the groups are ready, the first student attacks the defender, followed immediately by the second student's attack. Susan attacks Bob with a ridgehand strike. The moment Bob has blocked it, Jim attacks with a slow front kick. The more proficient Bob is at maintaining a clear and flowing mind, the better he will block one attack and be ready for whatever follows.

Whenever I teach this drill to a new group of students, I find they become increasingly competent after only a couple of classes and maintain their skill even as they increase the speed of their attacks. As with the first drill, they have problems only when they clutter their minds with anticipation. If they do become distracted they need only to let the distraction dissolve calmly. It's important they do not become frustrated or angry at themselves, since these emotions focus unwanted attention on the distraction. When these unwanted thoughts bubble to the surface, the students should just allow their minds to return calmly to the unobstructed, free-flowing state.

Ambiance

The mushin drills should be practised in a quiet atmosphere where the students are not allowed to talk. Eliminate distractions such as radios and observers, in order that the students can achieve and maintain a relaxed physical and mental state. This may seem an unrealistic environment, but when the drill is new to most people it requires maximum concentration. In time, students will be able to experience mushin in any environment, but in the beginning the exercise requires a high degree of control and the cooperation of all participants.

Applying mushin in its purest form means giving no thought to your opponent or yourself. Although you are ready, you have no specific technique in mind and are making no value judgements. Your attacks and blocks aren't executed consciously, but are led by your subconscious mind.

Bruce Lee referred to mushin as "it." When asked how he would fight if his life were at stake, Lee replied that he would probably hurt the assailant badly, possibly kill him. If that happened and he were to stand trial, he would say he was not responsible for his actions because he had acted without conscious thought. He would plea that he had not killed the assailant—"it" had.

8

MENTAL PREPAREDNESS

"BE ALERT—WHAT THE WORLD NEEDS IS MORE LERTS."

THAT POSTER HAS BEEN taped to the police station locker room for a long time. It's mostly ignored now, except by new recruits seeing it for the first time and by those unknown but ever-present graffiti artists. But those first two words should never be ignored: "BE ALERT."

Unfortunately, in today's city streets danger is all around us—and most people fail to see the signs until it's too late. Their eyes may be open but their naiveté blinds them to potential dangers.

How about you? Perhaps you've been studying karate for a couple of years or more. Have you cultivated your awareness along with your finely tuned fighting skill? Are you alert to what is happening around you, or are you like most people, who walk along oblivious to nearly everything around them?

Let's say you've lived in your neighbourhood for several years and routinely make a four-block walk to the grocery store. You've walked this stretch hundreds of times without any problem, and as a result, you now take this stroll with no more concern than if you were walking from your TV to the bathroom. You're so caught up in your routine that you function blindly, completely unaware of your surroundings.

A new resident in your neighbourhood may be just as oblivious to any danger signs. Because everything is so new to him, he sees only the beautiful, tree-lined streets and trendy shops. He's so caught up in the forest that he would be unable to see danger even if it lurked behind every tree.

56

Whether you're new to your area or have simply grown complacent in your routine, your survival may be based only on your good luck. If you've not yet been harassed, taunted, pushed, punched, robbed or worse, be thankful; you've escaped only because it hasn't been in the cards. Sad to say, such misfortune is in the cards for hundreds of thousands of victims in North America every year. True, some dangerous situations are unavoidable. But too often people become victims through being too casual, too routine, or too blasé. In other words, they are not mentally prepared.

BE LIKE THE BOY SCOUTS

A good Boy Scout is always prepared, and so should be the good martial artist. Most people study the fighting arts to develop confidence through learning to defend themselves. Others study because they are interested in learning a skill from another culture, and still others are motivated primarily by the benefits of physical fitness. Whatever your reason, your involvement with the fighting arts doesn't end when you walk out the door of your school.

It's ridiculous to go to all the effort of earning a black belt and then walk around with your head in your workout bag, completely oblivious to the dangers that may be around you. Mental preparation is part of your development. Without it you have no awareness, no idea of when danger is near, not even a glimmering of its possibility.

To be prepared, you must be alert to your surroundings. Your awareness must be as finely tuned as your backfist and sidekick, because without it, you may never get to use these techniques you have worked so long to perfect.

As a warrior, you need to be alert and prepared for any danger in your environment.

Christensen

THE FOUR STAGES

There are four stages of alertness and awareness, ranging from complete unawareness to total concentration and absorption in a situation. While some people instinctively fluctuate between one stage and another as the situation dictates, others, including many martial artists, may fail to make the shift or even sense the need. This can be dangerous, even fatal.

Stage One

This mental stage is the most rudimentary and the most dangerous: you go about your day not recognizing or comprehending that there are dangers around you. Most victims of crime fall into this trap. They are so caught up in their daily routine that they are oblivious to all else, drifting around in a fog as though trusting to a little guardian angel sitting on their shoulders. And so they leave their cameras on their dashboards, their ten-speed bicycles unattended on the sidewalk, and their car motors running as they dash into a convenience store.

Stage One can actually encourage attack. Studies have shown that potential victims share a walk, an attitude and a general demeanour that target them for victimization. They walk timidly, as if afraid of everyone and everything around them. Thus they are usually considered easy prey by muggers and other criminals.

Stage Two

Stage Two is one of caution: although there is no specific danger, you sense a need for relaxed alertness. Knowledgeable people switch into this stage at night as they walk to their car across an unlit parking lot. They are keenly aware of areas that cannot be seen, such as behind parked cars, garbage cans and dark alleyways.

Martial artists who are mentally prepared are aware of everything around them. They know what is "normal" in a given situation and therefore their attention is instantly drawn to whatever is unusual. Although not overly concerned about being mugged, they recognize the possibility in these circumstances, and therefore tune their senses to a higher level of perception. They continually look and listen, giving serious attention to any instinctive impressions of danger.

Stage Three

There's a definite perception of threat in this stage. If you are mentally prepared, you have recognized the signs of danger, and have begun to think in terms of tactics and develop a plan.

Some typical situations:

● You're the only shopper in a late-night convenience store as two punks enter, their portable stereo blasting. They laugh hilariously as one of them holds the arms of the only clerk while the other grabs a case of beer. Then they see you.

- As you and your date walk back to your car from a late movie, you round the corner and see that your car door is open and someone is going through the glove compartment.

- You've been sitting having a beer with a friend in a tavern where two large, drunk men are shooting a noisy game of pool. When you get up to use the restroom, one of them steps in your path and looks at you defiantly.

At Stage Three, your brain is racing because you know a confrontation is likely. You are aware of the problem and all your surroundings: front, rear, sides, the presence of other people, passing cars and so on. As you analyze the data, you formulate a plan based on your experience, training and common sense.

Stage Four

It's begun. The fight is on. Before you're able to leave the store, the two punks rush you; the car prowler hears your footsteps, scrambles from the car and advances toward you; the drunk in the bar swings his pool cue.

At Stage Four you react instantaneously. You can do this only when you have been alert to the danger signs. Thus, you are able to flow easily into your plan of action.

A person walking about in Stage One will be in danger in such situations because he hasn't been alert to anything going on around him. By the time he's noticed what's happening, it's too late. It will take him too long to make the transition from Stage One to Stage Four to react effectively.

A person who has been in Stage Two (caution and alertness) can more easily move up one or two stages in an instant: see the problem, decide what to do and take swift action. It's impossible, however, for someone functioning at Stage One to gain control of a dangerous situation if he doesn't even know the situation exists.

PANIC OR PARALYSIS

A person who reacts with panic or is paralyzed with fear is unable to respond to the threat. Faced with the car prowler he may "freeze," unable to move. Or he may run off in blind terror, leaving his date to fend for herself.

There have been cases where this has occurred to highly trained martial artists. They kick and grapple ineffectually, their practised techniques reduced to nothing more than wild flailing. They may fall to the ground, weakened with fear and unable to function.

This is most likely to happen to a person in Stage One, that mental state in which you are oblivious to danger or the possibility of danger. When suddenly thrust face to face with it, the Stage One mind cannot make the transition in time, if at all. The shock of danger is then so traumatic, so completely unexpected, that your mind shuts down and you cannot react appropriately.

Your mind should always be in Stage Two, except when you're safely in the comfort of your own home and a few other places where you are absolutely sure you're free of danger. This alertness gives you an edge and actually discourages attack. The more you are prepared to defend yourself, the less likely you will need to.

THE FREEWAY CREEP

Let's examine a situation to see how two people, one chronically in Stage One and you, a Stage Two person, handle an angry motorist. The motorist feels you've violated his space somehow and takes advantage of the red light to leap from his car and stomp up to your door.

The person in Stage One sitting in his car, wonders why this guy is so angry and why he's shouting and making terrible threats. The Stage One man laboriously climbs from his car and stands directly behind his door where the angry man can easily slam it into his knees. He then realizes he's forgotten his baseball hat, turns his back on the angry motorist and reaches across his seat to fetch it.

With his hat now perched on his head, Mr. Stage One leans back against his car and asks the guy with the beet-red face why he's so upset. This infuriates the man even more and he begins to clench his fists. Of course this has gone unnoticed by Mr. Stage One because his attention has been distracted by a fine-looking lady walking by.

The angry man suddenly becomes quiet, and this change also goes unnoticed. The Stage One man is so oblivious to everything, he doesn't even see the big, hairy fist speeding on a collision course toward his jaw.

Exaggeration? No, it isn't. Although it doesn't always end with a punch, there are many people, including those trained in the fighting arts, who somehow make it through the day as if they were in a fog they can't see out of.

You, however, are highly trained physically and mentally. Skillful and alert, you operate in Stage Two, a level where you are keenly aware of your surroundings. You immediately note the man scrambling from his car and striding angrily towards you. You are quickly out of your car, apologizing for any offence you may have given. Sometimes a quick apology, even if you're not sure what it is you may have done, will defuse a situation. But let's say in this case it doesn't work.

The angry man's car is directly in front of yours and another car has pinned you in from the rear, so there is no ready escape from the scene. Being aware of the cars passing by in the next lane, you ask the guy to step over to the curb. If this situation were to erupt into a fight, one or both of you might be struck by passing cars. Although you realize your request could be construed by an antagonist as a challenge to fight, the risk of getting run over is greater.

As the angry motorist moves toward the curb, you take note of his age, physical size, probable physical condition, the manner in which he carries himself and the possibility of a concealed weapon. You also note the presence of anyone else in his car, of any pedestrians and environmental objects such as telephone poles, fire hydrants and traffic signs.

You make these observations quickly because you want to concentrate primarily on the man. You're aware of distancing as you step to the curb and stop a little more than arm's reach from him. You understand the action/reaction principle (see Chapter 9) and want to give yourself time to react should he become aggressive.

You concentrate on the man's eyes as you politely listen to him, but your peripheral vision takes in his hands and feet. You know that most people look at a target before they hit it. If the motorist is about to choke you, he'll look at your neck first; if he's thinking of kicking you in the groin, he'll look there. By being alert to his gaze, you will minimize the possibility of a surprise attack.

During your entire contact with the man, you are cool, calm and in control. Often a calm demeanour in the face of someone who has lost control of his is enough to bring him down. Even if this fails, a calm mind will enable you to think clearly and accurately assess all the information gained from your senses. When you're in control of yourself you'll be better able to control someone else. If the situation does suddenly erupt into violence, your calm mind will allow you to react with mushin.

The Sixth Sense

Besides being completely aware of everything about the man and your immediate surroundings, you're also monitoring your feelings about the situation. Often we speak of having a premonition or "sixth sense." Bruce Lee argued that the so-called sixth sense was nothing more than a heightened awareness of the five senses. Whatever it is, or however it's called, a premonition is a valid feeling and should be considered.

You won't experience this feeling if you are oblivious to what's going on around you. All animals, our human ancestors included, developed this instinct as a means of survival in a hostile world. Over the years, we seem to have lost this instinct, or buried it deep within our unconscious, especially those of us who are fortunate enough to live in a relatively insulated world, virtually free from danger or bodily harm.

To be a complete martial artist—a warrior, if you will—you need to develop this instinct. You'll need to be alert to the dangers of your environment. You'll need to develop an awareness and a gut feeling that you can trust. And you can, but only through constant effort and a realization of its necessity.

This is what we mean by mental preparedness. In the case of our angry motorist, maintaining your alertness throughout your contact with him will prepare you should he become combative. Even if you find you can control him through your speech and manner, you should continue to monitor him as you both return to your cars. Do not drop your mental guard just because he appears to have recognized the stupidity of his actions. As a policeman, I have investigated many situations where someone has walked back to his car after apologizing or being defeated in a fight, only to return with a gun. Maintain your Stage Three state of mind until you're both back in your cars and you've turned right and he has gone left. Then and only then can you return to your Stage Two state of mind.

9

PRINCIPLES

WHAT ARE PRINCIPLES?

WEBSTER'S DICTIONARY defines a principle as a "basic truth," which is a good definition of the three principles discussed in this chapter: the distraction principle, the high/low principle, and the action/reaction principle. Whether we call them truths or rules of combat, they exist today, they existed yesterday, and you can count on their being here tomorrow. They cannot be ignored.

Gravity, that invisible power that keeps things clinging to the earth, is a principle. If you toss an apple into the air, it's true that it will fall back to the earth. But even though the truth doesn't change, there are a variety of ways to throw the ball: overhand, underhand, behind your back or through your legs. No matter what type of technique you use to get the ball airborne, the principle of gravity will bring it back down.

As a martial artist, you need to understand the principles of combat and use their truths to make your fighting more successful, whether in competition or in the street. There are hundreds, perhaps thousands of techniques that apply the various combat principles. Remember, you can't change the rules, but you can be as creative as you want with the techniques.

THE DISTRACTION PRINCIPLE

The principle of distraction is based on the fact that the mind can focus on only one thing at a time. Even though the mind can quickly shift gears and change its focus, it still requires an instant to do so. But for a fighter who understands the distraction principle, an instant may be all that is needed to accomplish an objective.

A Painful Analogy

Let's say you've just whacked your bare shin into the metal frame of your bed and you're screaming and hopping about in agony. Your hands are clutching the injured leg as waves of hot, nauseating pain spread throughout your entire body. All your attention is riveted on that tiny spot from where the pain is emanating.

At this exact moment, a person standing a few feet away throws a small ball to you. Do you think you'll catch it?

The probability of your failing the catch is quite high. In fact, there's a good chance the ball will bounce off your forehead without your even trying to intercept it. If you think otherwise, you've never slammed your bare shin into hard, cold steel. When all of your being is focused on the pain, there's not enough time to move your thoughts from your shin to the act of catching a ball.

This example may be extreme, but it nonetheless illustrates how the mind can have difficulty switching focus. As a fighter, you want to use this principle to take advantage of your opponent. And since there's not always a bed frame for him to bang into, you need to provide him with situations that will distract his mind.

Faking

Faking is a common tactic that uses the distraction principle. Faking creates a mistaken belief in your opponent's mind that a specific attack or movement is taking place, while in reality you are preparing another technique to hit a different target. When you thrust your open palm toward your opponent's face, he thinks, if only momentarily, his face is going to be struck. He reacts to this belief by initiating an evasive movement or some type of block. It's at this exact moment of distraction that you drive a hard kick into his groin.

The Faked Mind

When you thrust your palm toward your opponent's face, there are a number of things going on in his mind. First, his eyes see the palm and send an "alert" message to his brain, which quickly computes the message to, "Yipes! A thrusting palm . . . Danger! Danger! I'd better do something." His brain must then choose from a number of possible responses—block, duck, run, or do nothing—and then send the chosen response to the appropriate muscles.

While your opponent's brain is busy, you fire your second technique in to score. Although his brain is proccessing the fake at a high rate of speed, your opponent must interrupt this process long enough to register the second attack: see it, recognize it and respond in some way. Before he's completed the process for the second attack, your technique has successfully landed.

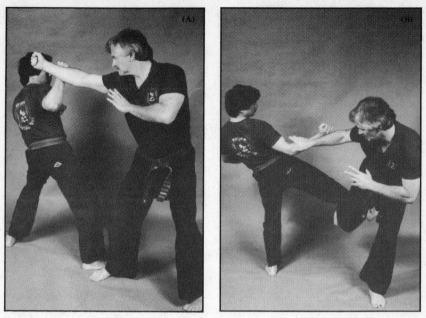

You throw a fake backfist to your opponent's head to draw his guard and attention up **(A)**. You then shuffle forward and scoop his leg out from under him, and he falls to the ground **(B)**.

There are at least three reasons why your second attack will score.

1. Your opponent's thinking process remains focused on the fake and his eyes haven't seen the other attack.
2. His mental process of intercepting the fake has been disrupted by the initial movement of your second technique, but a complete recognition hasn't taken place.
3. His mind has recognized your second technique, but has not set a reaction into motion.

Why a Fake Fails

Your fake may not get the reaction you want because it doesn't look real. If your opponent doesn't believe it, he won't respond to it. Basically, a fake is a partially executed technique, such as a backfist or a sidekick that is thrown just far enough to elicit a response but not so far that it makes contact. In some circumstances a twitch of the shoulders or an arch of the eyebrows will get a reaction. Usually, however, the fake needs to travel close to a target in order to trigger a mental and physical response.

Faking the Intoxicated Person

One common reason fakes fail in a street confrontation is that the recipient's mind may be dulled through the influence of alcohol or drugs. A drunk has difficulty seeing, recognizing and responding to fakes since his vision, thinking process and muscle response are all impaired. It takes an intoxicated person longer to see the threat and much longer for the brain to receive and register it.

This doesn't mean you can't fake someone in this condition; however, the technique should be modified. One simple method is to throw the fake slower so it can be perceived and registered in the intoxicated mind. The sluggish mind needs more time to react. If a fake is thrown too quickly, it may not register in your opponent's mind, or he may ignore the movement.

Another method is to throw the technique so that it blocks the opponent's sight. For example, thrust your palm into his face, hold it there for just an instant so his drunken attention is focused on your hand, and then slam your real attack into an exposed target. In this case you're giving him plenty of time to focus his intoxicated eyes and brain on the fake, thus giving yourself time to deliver the second attack.

Distraction and the Grappling Arts

Grappling arts, such as jujitsu, aikido, chin-na and wrestling are most effective when there's an element of surprise. An opponent with any intelligence at all won't stand motionless while you apply a wrist lock or a takedown technique. If your intentions are too obvious, your opponent will stiffen his arm, jerk it away or just punch you in the nose. To attack successfully with a grappling technique, the opponent's thought process must first be distracted.

Soften Him First

Most grappling arts incorporate striking techniques to distract or "soften" an opponent. By first kicking him in the groin, you'll definitely soften him for the follow-up armlock.

You simultaneously block your opponent's blow and kick him in the groin (A). With his attention directed at his pain, you can easily apply an arm lock (B, C).

The concept is simple. When your opponent throws a punch, his thought process is divided between his punch and its intended target. By blocking the punch and simultaneously kicking him in the groin, you'll distract his thoughts long enough to apply a grappling technique. If you've ever been soundly kicked in the groin, or even gently tapped, you can appreciate that it will take your opponent a moment to shift his thoughts from that location to the technique you're applying on his arm.

There are some karate people who scorn the grappling arts, believing them ineffective, since one cannot apply a wrist lock on a fast backfist. There are jujitsu masters who possess this ability. However, if you're not a master, you'll have greater success with your grappling techniques when you understand and apply the distraction principle.

Using Distraction to Re-apply a Grappling Technique

Most grappling techniques have what is called a lock-in feature. Generally this occurs at the end of the technique where your opponent's joint, muscles or tendons are pushed to their maximum and the pain is at its greatest. It's at this lock-in point where the technique is strongest and the most difficult to escape from. For the most part, without this lock-in there is little possibility of controlling your opponent through pain. Usually, your opponent will resist your hold at a point just short of where the technique locks in. Since you've not yet applied maximum pain, your technique disintegrates into a muscle-versus-muscle contest, a situation you want to avoid—especially if your opponent is stronger than you.

To prevent this from happening, you need to be aware of his mental process. Let's say you've grabbed his arm—one hand on his wrist, the other on his upper arm—and plan to bend his arm at the elbow and apply a joint lock on his wrist. Just as you begin to bend his arm, he bunches his fist and tenses his arm muscles, thus preventing you from completing the hold. His thoughts are on his stiff arm and trying to keep you from bending it. The more you struggle to gain control, the harder he tenses and the greater his mental focus.

To get control, you need to remove his attention from the arm and transfer his focus elsewhere. A technique called "crab bites" is a subtle yet painful method that works just about every time. When you feel his arm tense, maintain your hold on his wrist and use the thumb and the index fingernail of your other hand to pinch the soft flesh of his armpit, or the vulnerable skin under his forearm. When he jerks in pain, you must immediately strike with your pinching hand against the inside of his elbow and bend his arm. It bends because you have momentarily diverted his mind from concentrating on stiffening his arm to a different location of pain. As a result, he is unable to maintain his strength. Since his distraction is brief, you need to get control quickly so that he doesn't re-focus his strength.

A similar situation may occur when you've locked your opponent in a hold but for some reason he starts to slip out of it. Perhaps your technique is weak, or your hands are sweaty, or the technique is ineffective on him. As he struggles to free himself from your grip, you need to divert his attention so that you can regain the hold or switch to a different one.

Using Distraction to Release Your Opponent's Hold

Distraction is an invaluable tool in breaking an opponent's grip on you, your clothing, or a weapon. The more you struggle to relax his grip, the greater he struggles to hold on. Whether he has a hold of your shirt front, is squeezing you in a headlock, or has locked his hand onto the handle of a knife, his physical strength and mental focus will increase the more you try to get him to let go. In fact, because of his narrow field of focus, especially in the case of a violent or mentally disturbed person, his physical strength can be extraordinary.

In addition to groin kicking and crab bites, other effective methods for distraction include:

- *Twisting a neck cord*
  Grasp a neck cord on either side of the neck with the thumb and index finger, and pinch and twist vigorously.

- *Thumbing the side of the eye*
  Push, not jab your thumb against the "crow's feet" on the outside of the eye.

- *Hair twisting*
  Grasp the hair on the sides of the head, just above the ears, or on the upper neck. Close your fingers into a tight fist and twist left or right.

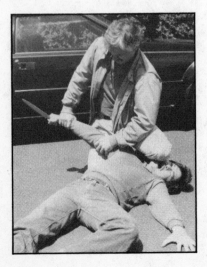

Hyperextending your opponent's elbow across your thigh will direct his attention to the pain in the joint, rather than on his weapon. He will eventually drop the knife.

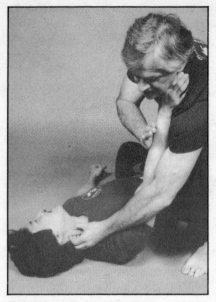 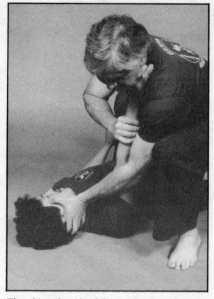

Twisting a neck cord: Grasp a neck cord with your thumb and index finger on either side of his neck, and pinch and twist vigorously.

Thumbing the side of the eye: Push and grind your thumb against the "crow's feet" on the outside of his eye.

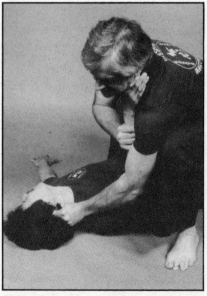

Hair twisting: Grasp the hair on the side of his head and close your fingers into a tight fist; then twist left or right.

An opponent is applying an arm bar on you **(A)**. You kick him in the groin to distract and soften him **(B)**. You then disengage his grasp **(C)**, reverse the hold and apply it on him **(D, E)**.

Another War Story

Police officers hate family fight calls. Domestic disputes are unpredictable, can be dangerous, and frequently involve violence against children. Such was the case when my partner and I responded to a call early one Sunday morning.

Even if the apartment door hadn't been ajar we could easily have heard the baby screaming and the man and woman shouting. As we stepped into the living room, the first thing we saw was a man lying face down on the sofa and a woman frantically pounding her fists on the guy's back. In one quick motion we sprang at her and pulled her, kicking and screaming, to the far side of the room.

"He's got my baby," she gasped, hysterical. "He's trying to crush it."

Confused, my partner and I looked back at the man who was still lying motionless, both arms hidden under him, face buried in a cushion with a baby's foot protruding from under his chest. A BABY'S FOOT!

Moving as one, my partner and I brushed the woman aside, grabbed the man and jerked him over onto his side. Almost incomprehensible to us was the sight of a naked baby, the man's arms tightly folded across its tiny chest and stomach. The man's eyes were glassy and heavy-lidded; the baby's face was frighteningly blue.

We tore desperately at the man's arms but the harder we pulled, the more he tightened his deadly grip on the baby. Pitting strength against strength only made matters worse. Changing tactics, I thrust my hand to the back of his head, grabbed a fistful of his hair and closed my hand into a tight fist.

As I rotated my hand 180 degrees, the man screamed and shot his hands toward the ripping pain. The baby rolled off his chest onto the sofa and was quickly scooped up by my partner. I maintained the hair hold for control while the handcuffs were locked onto his wrists.

THE HIGH/LOW PRINCIPLE

The distraction principle moves your opponent's concentration from point A to point B so that you have a clear path to attack point A. This is based on the idea that the brain can focus on only one thing at a time.

The principle of high/low uses this same idea but with different techniques to get different results. When you use the high/low principle, you want your opponent's thinking process to focus on a high point of his body while you attack a low point. Or, you want his attention diverted *down* while you attack *up*. An example would be a low roundhouse kick to the shin followed by a backfist to the ear.

By first kicking his shin, you draw his attention to a low point on his body. Just glimpsing the initial motion of your kick sends his attention downward, while the painful contact of your foot against his shin completely focuses his mind there. It's at this exact moment that you strike high. With his thoughts, his pain and possibly his eyes all concentrated low, you've gained a moment to strike elsewhere.

An effective tournament technique is executed by faking a front kick to the groin **(A)**, and then rolling the leg into a roundhouse kick **(B)** and scoring to the head **(C)**.

A simple street technique using the high/low principle is to whip a hard roundhouse into the opponent's knee **(A)** and then slam a high backfist to his face **(B)**.

Kicking to Miss

It isn't even necessary to land the first attack in order for the high/low principle to work. This tactic is especially useful in tournament competition, where attacks to your opponent's legs are not allowed. A double roundhouse kick can be executed by faking to the groin with the first kick, and kicking to the head with the second. Or, you can throw a fake roundhouse kick to the head and, as your opponent moves to block or react to it, you can move in quickly for a leg sweep. Whether you hit or fake with the first technique, your objective is to move your opponent's mind in the opposite direction of your second attack.

Multiple High/Low Attacks

The high/low principle works well when you are throwing multiple attacks. By hitting high, low, high and low again, you overwhelm your opponent by not letting his mind catch up with the point of attack. Your kick connects with his knee and his thoughts race downward. Instantly your backfist smacks against his ear and his mind races toward his head. But just as his attention arrives at the pain in his ear, you drive a hard punch into his lower abdomen.

He's a bit sluggish now as his mind makes its way toward his stomach. Then you add the cherry to the pudding with a hard ridgehand strike across the bridge of his nose. When these techniques are coming fast and furious, it's difficult, if not impossible, for your opponent's mind to keep up with them. He will block desperately to ward off the blows, thereby creating more openings for you to hit.

ACTION/REACTION PRINCIPLE

The action/reaction principle is based on the fact that action is faster than reaction. Say you're standing within striking range of your opponent and she decides to ram a fist into your nose. Before she moves, there are a few things that occur within her brain that you're unaware of. First, there is her decision to hit you, a thought process she can execute without moving her body or exhibiting any facial expressions that give away her intention. Secondly, she can decide how she intends to do so, also a mute process. Lastly, she and only she has the luxury of knowing at which moment she's going to do it.

The first you're aware that she's up to no good is when you see her fist rushing toward your face. Since she's been standing within striking range, she doesn't need to make a forward movement, which would alert you to her intentions. She's already decided what, how and when and you're forced to react at the last moment before her fist scores.

Without warning, you're in the less than desirable position of reacting to her action. To react, your eyes must perceive her fist and send an alert message to your brain. Your brain must digest the message, which involves decoding it, deciding how to react, and then sending a command to the proper muscles to duck or block. Unfortunately, your reaction is too late and you've

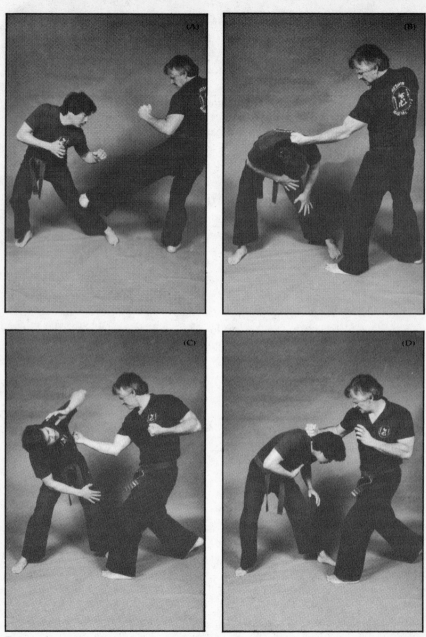

Drive a fast side kick into his knee **(A)** and backfist his head as he reaches toward the pain **(B)**. Punch his ribs **(C)** as he grabs his head and follow with a hammerfist to his neck as he covers his ribs **(D)**.

already been struck. And it matters little if you're a black belt and the attacker is a white belt: action is always faster than reaction, regardless of the skill involved.

Standing Too Close

Standing too close is a common fault in classroom sparring, tournament competition and, most dangerous of all, street confrontations. A typical bar fight usually begins with two people standing chest to chest and screaming

insults at each other. They double their fists, shout profanity and even bounce their chests against each other, as though engaged in some mandatory, pre-fight ritual. It looks silly and it's extremely dangerous. Since action is faster than reaction and they're within arm's reach of each other, the first one to throw a punch will have a ninety-nine percent chance of success.

In a street situation you should never allow yourself to stand so close that you don't have enough time to react. Stay at least an arm's length away from your opponent, more if you have the slightest hint that he's a kicker.

Give yourself enough space so that you gain reaction time. When your opponent attacks, he must move his entire body to close the gap, thus giving you an extra instant in which to defend yourself.

Sparring Range

You also want to be aware of reaction time when you're sparring in your school or in a tournament. Squaring off with your lead hand against your opponent's is unrealistic training and creates a dangerous habit that will continue in the street. Always train to keep out of kicking range so that you have time to react.

Of course, when you're out of range you'll also have to close the distance when you attack. This is why you train so hard on your footwork, fakes and combinations: so that you can close the distance sucessfully.

Action/Reaction and the Armed Assailant

The most dangerous self-defence situation is having to defend yourself against an armed assailant. Some books and magazines illustrate a number of techniques that can be used against a gun, usually fancy kicks and judo flips. These may be effective, but they should never be used as an initial defence.

Your primary concern when facing a firearm is to get your body out of the line of the bullet's trajectory and to get hold of the armed hand or the weapon itself. Those kicks and flips are secondary because, if you don't get your body out of the way first and secure the weapon so that it's pointed away from you, you're not going to be able to do anything else anyway.

Applying the Principle

The actions of moving your body from the bullet's path and restraining the weapon are made simpler when you apply the action/reaction principle. First, however, recall the distraction principle—the fact that the mind can focus on only one thing at a time. You need to be aware of where your assailant's attention is directed and to keep his mind occupied so that you can initiate your action. If he's talking, you know his mind is tied up with what he's saying. If he's silent, then you need to occupy his mind by talking so he's listening to what you're saying. Then when you make your physical move, he'll have to shift gears mentally before he can react. This will slow him down.

Your body will need to be close to his and you'll want your hands close to the weapon. As well, you'll need to be able to twist your body quickly out of the line of fire.

The most important factor to consider before you ever attempt to disarm someone is to be absolutely convinced the assailant is going to shoot you. Unfortunately, only you can make that decision. You'll make it based on what he's saying, how he's acting, and that sixth sense we call "gut feeling." When all of these indicate he's going to shoot, then you will need to call upon all your physical skills as well as your understanding of the mental process.

Most, if not all fighting tactics fall under one or more of these three principles. To be a smart fighter, you need to understand why your favourite strategies work. Such concepts as faking, angling, broken rhythm, jamming, counter-punching and rushing all fall under one or more of the principles we've discussed. When you know how a tactic is likely to affect your opponent's mind, you'll be able to create more techniques using these principles.

The bottom line is that when two people are equal physically, the smarter one, the fighter with more knowledge of himself and his opponent, will be victorious.

Talk to the gunman or try to get him to talk so his attention is focused on the words (A). When the moment is right, quickly rotate your waist and simultaneously grab his wrist, pushing the gun aside (B). Twist the gun back toward him and to the outside of his shoulder (C). Step in the direction you are twisting and take him to the ground (D). Continue to twist his hand until he releases the weapon.